H. DOUGLAS KNUST

Man Stuff - Things a Young Man Needs to Know

kindle direct publishing

Contents

VII   Clothing & Stuff

Preface

When my son was in seventh grade, I saw a need for some kind of youth organization that ALL young men could belong to – even those who were not athletic. I started the Explorers Club, a boys service club for 6-8th grade Chamberlain Public School and St. Joseph's Indian School students, in the fall of 2001. Since then, over 350 young men have worked to raise over $145,000 for their school and community which has helped fund over $735,000 in projects for the area.

This money has helped construct a new baseball field (with scoreboard) and new soccer field; purchase new playground equipment at two parks, new slides and equipment for the municipal swimming pool and A/V equipment and an AED device for the school; construct a fishing pier in the municipal campground, a new picnic shelter, and a community Frisbee golf course; and purchase trees, 60 new flag poles for community flag park, and equipment at Veterans Park. They have given financial support to the local "Meals on Wheels" and "Relay for Life" programs in addition to many other things.

They volunteer for an impressive list of service projects including cleaning school grounds, assisting with Veterans Day programs, assisting with sports tournaments, serving meals at high school athletic banquet, hosting Halloween parties for mentally handicapped, and performing various chores for elderly community members. They raise money for numerous people fighting health issues. They truly are the "go-to" organization for service and help in the community.

The group has won the South Dakota Middle Level Educators "Friend of Education" Award (2002); Chamberlain Public School District "Friend of Education" Award (2002); School Administrators of South Dakota "Helping Hands" Award (2002); Chamberlain-Oacoma Area Chamber of Commerce Volunteer of the Year Award (2009 & 2016).

The Explorers (30-45 members each year) conduct their weekly meeting each Thursday morning at 7:30 AM. I prepare the agenda and the elected officers conduct their meeting. They plan their activities and report on recent events.

The Explorers go on two trips annually. They trek to Pierre (South Dakota's capitol) to meet our governor and various constitutional officers. They are introduced to our legislature and tour various museums and agencies in Pierre. Then they cap each school year with a trip to Minneapolis, Kansas City or Denver to see a couple of MLB baseball games.

They host a middle school dance each year. As the DJ for that dance each year, I am reminded of the awkwardness of this age, especially when it comes to dances!

In 2014, I began a segment at each of their weekly meetings that I called "Man Stuff". I took a life lessons topic that I thought would be interesting to the young men and something that might serve them well growing up. It soon proved to be the highlight of the meetings. The guys really enjoyed it.

The chapters of this book come from those "Man Stuff" lessons. The lessons range from life skills (how to tie a tie, how to shake hands, the importance of being on time, etc.) to good to know skills (how to jump start a car, men's room etiquette, and how to wear cologne). This is not the entire list of Man Stuff topics. (Perhaps the others will come in Man Stuff 2.0!)

Of the awards I have been fortunate to receive during my adult life, none compares to the reward of working with the Explorers Club. For more than 19 years now, the organization has served our community and our school. While my name may be on them, the awards belong to the young men in the organization.

My reward is the relationships that I have forged working with these young men. Many are now married and have kids of their own. I am often sought out at community events of after church service by former Explorers who just want to say hi or reflect on their time in the club.

I look forward to these meetings each Thursday. It is my privilege to work with these young men and I am so proud of their work in the community.

Acknowledgement

Thanks to my family for their support of this book and the Explorers group. Thanks to my wife, Judy, who supports everything I do in every way she can. Thanks to my daughter, Rachel Millard, who is the writer in the family and helped with editing. Thanks to my son, Alex Knust, the artist in the family, who created the cover and back of the book. Thanks to my daughter, Sarah Knust, who is the enthusiastic, positive force in our family and who always makes everything more fun.

Thanks to my life-long friend, Craig Kirsch, the best writer I know, for advice, inspiration and support along the way.

Thanks to Debbie Johnson (Chamberlain principal when I started Explorers; later superintendent of Chamberlain Schools; also the mother of three sons) for supporting the Explorers Club and my efforts with the Explorers in every way possible. There would be no Explorers Club if not for Debbie's unending support. Debbie nominated the Explorers for several awards and has always supported in so many ways.

Thanks to Rocky Almond for his help in getting the Explorers Club up and running. Rocky is an educator in every sense of the word!

Thanks to the Chamberlain-Oacoma community for supporting all of the Explorers' causes. I am grateful that so many recognize that an investment in the Explorers Club is an investment in our future. This only happens in a caring community.

Special thanks to the parents of Explorers who have been so supportive, have chaperoned so many events and have driven to so many venues!

Thank you to each of the Explorers (listed in the back of this book) who have taught me more about life than I could ever teach them. It's been a fun ride!

I

Relationships & Stuff

1

Shake Down!

I'm going to share a lesson worth knowing – first impressions count in life. And one of the most important first impressions we give a person is through our handshake. But just how important is a handshake? Former President John F. Kennedy knew that the handshake made the first impression of him to leaders around the world so he commissioned a study to determine the best way to shake hands. He knew it was important to get it right!

Shaking hands sounds like an easy exercise. Unfortunately, there are quite a few ways a handshake can go wrong. From a sweaty hand to a bone-crushing grip, handshakes come in all shapes and sizes - and only the best will hit the right note.

When to Shake

Here's the golden rule: if you are meeting someone new or reconnecting with someone you're previously acquainted with, extend your hand for a handshake. Traditionally, the person who is older or in a position of higher authority should, generally, initiate a handshake. For example, at a job interview, the interviewer typically extends his or her hand first. Remember to always follow the lead of the person extending their hand.

However, not everyone knows or understands etiquette, so it is not rude to extend your hand first. This presents a great opportunity to make that great first impression. People will be impressed that a young person is confidant enough to introduce himself with a handshake. Feel free to initiate if you feel it is appropriate (and it almost always is!).

Hygiene

Your hand should be clean and not wet or clammy. If your hand is dirty, just note you're your hands are not clean and offer your apologies.If it is wet or clammy, try to inconspicuously wipe it on your pants.

Eye Contact

Making eye contact is almost as important as the hands in the handshake. Your eyes convey the most about you in an introduction. Looking down to the ground tells the person that you are shy, nervous and even untrustworthy. Avoiding eye contact is behavior typically seen in someone who has done something wrong and feels ashamed of guilty. (See the chapter *The Eyes Have It.*)

Looking the person in the eyes conveys interest and engagement. **Always you look a person in the eyes when you shake**

their hand.

Offer a sincere smile to show you are happy to be where you are and who you are with. Be sure to square you shoulders and face the other person so you don't give the impression of a "fly by" handshake suggesting you have other places to be.

Use a firm grip

Your handshake should be firm but not bone-crushing. A soft grip signals that you are weak of character or not really interested in the person with whom you are shaking hands. If you get a weak grip from the other person, give them a slight squeeze, which may cue them to grip more firmly.

A firm grip, on the other hand, shows confidence, strength and enthusiasm. Don't overdo it as a grip that is overly strong can appear arrogant.

Don't be too hurried

A handshake should be inviting, not rushed. When you rush a handshake you often get caught in that embarrassingly halfhearted position where neither person is really gripping properly. Bring your hand out with your fingers straight and your thumb high and make sure you do not grip until the person's thumb is firmly locked next to yours.

You should also not be too hasty in letting go. Hold on for long enough to show the person that you are excited to meet them. The typical handshake lasts just a few seconds. Take your cue from the other person.

Don't shake too much

Despite the fact that we call it a "handshake", we aren't really "shaking" hands. It's more like a handgrip with a few "pumps" rather than shakes. The shake is up and down and usually not more than three times. Try to maintain eye contact and smile throughout.

Too much shaking is just weird. It can signal over-excitement or even desperation.

Make correct use of the left hand

On most occasions, a single-handed handshake is appropriate. However, on certain occasions the double handed shake will help convey to the other person that they are special. You can wrap your left hand around the other person's wrist or bottom of their hand when shaking. This type of hand shake would be reserved for that long-lost uncle or another person to whom you feel a more significant attachment.

It is likely not appropriate when introducing yourself for the first time to a new individual to whom you do not share close ties. It may seem a little enthusiastic.

If you choose to use both hands, you can use the left hand to touch the other person on the shoulder or elbow region. If you are shaking hands to say goodbye to someone you can use your left hand to pat them on the upper back as they walk away.

What to say?

If you are being introduced to someone new, say their name aloud to reinforce that you know their name. Call them by their name and don't use lazy substitutes like "mate", "brother" or "dude." People love to hear their own name.

Sometimes you can get a name wrong. Many names sound alike (Aiden and Hayden). If you're not sure, this is the time to get it right.

If it someone you know, a warm greeting is appropriate. Instead, you may choose to start the conversation with some initial small talk, such as a question about their life. (See *Beautiful Day, Isn't It?* later in this section.)

Who are you again?

Remind people of your name as soon as you shake their hand,

don't assume they know your name even if you have previously met them.

If you have met a person before try to give them a little reminder as you shake their hand. You could say something like, "Robert Smith. Great to see you again John." This will help to put them at ease and hopefully make the meeting a little more streamlined.

The handshake is a solid part of modern American life and culture. People of all races, shapes, sizes and status use the handshake as a way to greet a person, make an agreement or say goodbye. Please remember though, these rules are for America. Other countries and cultures have different handshake customs and/or different means of personal introduction.

2

The "Bro Hug"

What is a "bro hug"? Well, it is not the embrace you give to grandma when you show up at her house for Thanksgiving dinner.

The "bro hug" is a hybrid handshake-hug that is typically used between two men to signify they're closer than a standard handshake. It is best reserved for use with close friends (and usually between men). It's appropriate in almost any setting (a night out, at the gym, or even at the office). It is usually done between 2 guys who know each other pretty well but don't want to go full-on "hug".

It's less formal than a handshake and more manly than a fist bump. But you have to be sure the other guy is into the bro hug too or he might think you're attacking him.

The bro hug is executed with hands extended but instead of shaking hands you smack them hard together. Drag the other bro towards you and do a full-arm wrap-around with one hand high and the other low – not 10 and 2 in clock positions, but say 7 and 2. That way your bro will be able to come in with his arms in opposite positions.

DO NOT go in for the hug with your arms at the same level, low or high. This forces your bro to take the opposite arm position, and you end up in a very strange hug - one bro's arms up high, the other bro's around his bro's waist, somewhat like junior high dancing. It also makes it really difficult to avoid your bro's face with your face.

End with three or four strong pats on the back (and an *optional* grunt or roar)!

Warning: Keep the lower half of your body AWAY from your Bro's lower half... otherwise it gets pretty awkward pretty fast!

3

Introducing...Me!

Introductions demonstrate confidence, and while important to people of all ages – it's not something typically associated with young men. So when young men choose to introduce themselves to adults, it makes a great impression. Let's go through a few of the basics.

Every strong introduction centers on a strong handshake (see later chapter "Shake Down!"). As you shake the other person's hand, however, it is what you say that sets the tone for the introduction and small talk and/or conversation that follows.

There may not be time for the post-introduction interaction but you do have a moment to make a lasting impression. That impression can be good, bad or unmemorable.

Here is an example of a strong introduction for a young man meeting an elected official:

"Good morning Governor Smith. My name is Doug Knust, and I'm an eighth grade student at Chamberlain Middle School. I am the secretary of the Explorers, a service club. I appreciate your taking time to meet us today."

Make the introduction relevant

In this example, the young person is offering a couple items of interest. He is telling his age, where he is from and that he is a leader in a service club. All are openings for conversation. He is also thanking the governor for his or her time. Gratitude toward any elected official for sharing their time is appropriate and memorable because they are seldom thanked for this.

Go beyond your name

This gives the person you are introducing yourself to something to ask to begin small talk or conversation.

Be original

Offer something that is unique and makes for good conversation. If you know something about or have something in common with the person you are introducing yourself to, bring it up in the introduction.

Think about it before the introduction

You are an interesting person. Think about what makes you interesting. Ask a friend or family member what they think makes you interesting.

Humor is great but be careful

Getting someone to laugh with you when you introduce yourself makes you memorable. But you don't want a joke or humor to fall flat. It's best to make fun of yourself rather than someone else.

Any of the topics for small talk (see the chapter ***The Art of Small Talk***) make good introduction lead-ins.

Remember to invoke a good, strong handshake as you introduce yourself. Make eye contact and don't hurry.

A young man who is confident enough to introduce himself to an adult will always make a strong and lasting impression. Even if you are not able to come up with something unique to reveal about yourself, you'll still be miles ahead of your peers!

4

Beautiful Day, Isn't It?

Do you keep trying to summon up the courage to talk to the cute girl in school but when you get around her all you can think to say is "hi"? Do you dread going somewhere new where you don't know anybody? Does the idea of walking into a party where you only know one person fill you with dread?

If you can learn the art of small talk, each of these social situations becomes much more comfortable.

Small talk is the back and forth conversation you have with strangers and acquaintances and even family members that you rarely see. Why do you need to know how to small talk?

Small talk leads you into deeper conversation where you really get to know someone. Think of it as the entry point from which all of your relationships begin.

So how do you gain the ability to make small talk with anyone? It starts with the courage to start the conversation. Find someone who looks like they feel awkward and go talk to them. You may feel self-conscious engaging a stranger in small talk, but most people are feeling as shy and insecure as you are. You are saving them from standing alone while they feel awkward and conspicuous when you take the initiative to talk to them

What do I say to them? Everyone's favorite subject is them self! Start by asking questions about their thoughts and interests. But as you do, keep these ideas in mind:

Ask open-ended questions

Avoid closed-ended questions that can be answered with a "yes" or "no". Open-ended questions will open the door to additional topics of conversation. They generate an interesting, dynamic conversation and encourage the person you're speaking with to share their thoughts and opinions.

Practice active listening

Look the person you are talking to in the eye. Give them some feedback - nod your head or smile. Let them know you're listening. It is much easier to ask relevant questions and remember details to bring up later if you're actively listening.

Put away your phone

We tend to pull out our phones when we're feeling uncomfortable or awkward in social situations, but nothing will destroy your conversational efforts more quickly. Few people will approach you if you're scrolling through your phone — and you send a plain message that you're not interested.

Show your enthusiasm

Small talk can be stressful. However, if you go into it with the right attitude, you can actually have fun. Treat these conversations as opportunities to learn more about other people. You never know whom you'll meet or what they'll have to share — so embrace the chance it'll be an amazing discussion.

Ideas for starting conversation

Use questions that begin with phrases like:

Tell me about...

What was the best part of...

How did you feel about...

What brought you to...

What's surprised you most...

How similar/different is that to...

Why...

...And ask about topics like this:

The Weather – what it's like where they are from, etc.

Sports – favorite teams(s), last night's game, etc.

Entertainment – Movies, TV shows, Local restaurants, Music, Books

Food – restaurants, current meal, etc

Work – what do they do, how did they get into that work, what do they like or dislike

Hobbies – what are their hobbies, how did they become interested in that, etc.

News – thoughts on current issues, local, regional, national

Family – married?, Kids?, siblings?, etc.

Travel – favorite place they've been, why?, upcoming trips, etc.

You can use any combination of the above ideas. You don't want the person to feel like it is an inquisition so add your thoughts as well.

Many people fail to remember that small talk is a necessary precursor to good conversation and to making new friends. Like anything, small talk gets easier with practice. You can practice anytime you are around people.

5

The Eyes Have It

Have you ever scanned a room and caught someone's eyes and quickly looked away? Eye contact is personal and sometimes uncomfortable social behavior, but man is it important. Many people, young and old, struggle with the skill of looking another person in the eye. In our culture, it is a very important social skill that every young man should work on.

Individuals who are able to make appropriate eye contact with others will be perceived as warm, personable, attractive, likable, skilled, competent, valuable, trustworthy, honest, sincere, confident and more powerful.

How to Make Eye Contact

We're not talking about staring someone down here. Eye contact should be welcoming and appropriate. When unwanted, eye contact can be staring, which makes people uncomfortable. So if you find someone will not return your eye contact after a couple of attempts, give it up.

When looking at another person, it's best to focus on one eye at a time and switch between them. Don't switch your gaze back and forth too frequently—just make it smooth and natural. It's fine to look away from someone when you're trying to gather your thoughts. It's quite appropriate to break eye contact and look away from someone as you recall a memory, consider something, or gather your thoughts about what you want to say next.

Eye contact and introductions

It is vitally important to make eye contact with someone when you are meeting them for the first time. As part of the "first impression" routine, you want to send the message to the other person that you are interested in them along with those qualities mentioned above.

Your eyes communicate with the other eyes

Eye contact improves the quality of interactions with others. Eye contact gives a sense of intimacy to your exchanges, and leaves the receiver of your gaze feeling more positive about your interaction and connected to you.

Eye contact is an important part of **active listening**. Make direct eye contact and a nod let the person know you are listening and engaged in the conversation. Think of how you feel when you're talking with someone and he's looking all around the room for someone else.

Eye contact and the ladies

Making eye contact is a great way to attract and hold the attention of ladies. Looking at a female directly, while also smiling, makes you appear more engaged and also may make you more attractive to her.

If a woman meets your eyes, don't be the first one to look away. Holding your gaze simply signals your confidence, which can be attractive to women. Ladies are, on average, better at making and holding eye contact than men are.

Our eyes reveal our thoughts and feelings.

You may have heard the old expression: "The eyes are the window to the soul." Maybe they are, maybe they're not. But the eyes do reveal a great deal about what we're really thinking and feeling from moment to moment.

Eye contact is truly a powerful tool for connecting with others, sharing our feelings, showing attention, and creating a bond.

6

There's No Place Like Home

When I left Chamberlain in the fall of 1978 to go to college in Omaha, NE, there is no way I ever thought I would come back to live. Eight years later, when my wife and I were expecting our first child, the idea of raising our kids in a small community started to have some appeal.

We had lived in Omaha and Des Moines, IA. Even though they were small cities, we saw some of the challenges of raising a family in that setting.

We were fortunate to have an opportunity to return home and join a family business. So that's what we did - return to a small, rural community to raise our family. We feel like it was a good decision.

I am proud of my home town and my home state. I find that the more I travel, the better both of them compare to anywhere else. I love to share fun facts about both Chamberlain and South Dakota with friends and visitors.

Every person should know some interesting facts about their hometown, their area and/or their state. It is admirable to be proud of your hometown and impressive to be able to recite such information.

In the Chamberlain-Oacoma, SD area, many of the jobs, especially for young people, are service jobs - many as restaurant servers. Many of the full time jobs are as fishing or hunting guides or similar positions.

These types of jobs are dependent on tips for some of the income. One is much more likely to get a good tip if you can engage your customer and provide some interesting insight to them.

So there may be both financial and personal reasons to know some interesting facts about your city, area or state.

Here are some examples of things you can research to be a resource for others. These topics all make great conversation starters as well. (See *Beautiful Day, Isn't It?* earlier in this section.)

- How did your hometown get its name?
- What is the history of your hometown? When was is founded? By whom? etc.
- What is the history of any attractions in your area?
- What is your hometown most famous for any why?
- What are some festivals or events people attend in your

area?
- What is the state bird, animal, flower, etc? Where can you find them?
- What is population of your hometown? State? Where does that rank?
- What are some fun facts about your hometown? State?

Once you start dropping a few of these pearls of information on people, you'll find they have questions for you and that the conversation is easy.

7

Lend a Hand, Take a Stand.

When I was in fourth grade, I was the shortest and skinniest person in my class. To be honest, I wasn't big enough to cast a decent shadow.

Yet, for some reason, the shortest (or just about the shortest) kid in fifth grade decided that he wanted to show me who was boss. Of course, being small himself he needed friends to help him, so he befriended the biggest kid in his class to intimidate me. This guy was huge and was a bit of a goon. I think he grunted once for "yes" and twice for "no". Regardless, he scared the hell out of me.

I don't remember what these two guys even did to me but I know I was terrified. I had to ride my bike right by the tormentor's house on my way home after school. I think he skipped out of school at noon each day so he could be positioned on his front yard and harass me when I went by his house.

I don't know how it ended or why. Perhaps I just started to grow and he found a different target. I did not know at the time that I was being bullied, but by today's definition, there is no doubt. It was stressful.

Forty-five years later, I was attending my wife's class reunion. My wife is a year older than me and my bully was in her class. He came over to me and told me that he was sorry for what he had done and that it had bothered him for some time. He just wanted to get it off his chest.

I forgave him. Forgiveness comes a little easier when you give it 45 years. And while I chose to forgive him, as I think back, it was a difficult time in my life.

What is bullying?

There are a few different types of bullying. Physical bullying is the stereotypical type that we usually see in movie scenes when someone trips someone else or pushes them up against a locker.

Verbal bullying is done using words either in person or online (cyber-bullying). It is quick, often done impulsively to evoke a response. Verbal is also easier to do without catching the attention of others. Examples include teasing, name calling, threats, intimidation, demeaning jokes, rumors, gossip, and slander.

Emotional bullying is calculated and manipulative and can be difficult to detect. It is usually executed by a group can be extremely damaging and traumatic. Emotional bullying is targeted at a person's sense of self and usually results in low or a complete lack of self-esteem. Examples of emotional bullying could be excluding someone from a group or purposely leaving them out of activities, threatening to hurt or harm someone, telling lies in order to hurt another person's reputation, and humiliating someone publicly. All of these can be done in-person or online.

Why does bullying exist?

People become bullies because they are insecure. They have

faults or weaknesses that they recognize but don't know how to deal with them so they try to bring others down to feel better about themselves.

But ultimately bullying does not exist because of the bully. Nor does it exist because of the bullied. Bullying exists because good people refuse to get involved. When onlookers allow a bully to work his threats, they enable the bully.

How do we stop bullying?

There is no teacher, principal, superintendent, police officer or elected official that can stop bullying, unless it is a teacher, principal, superintendent, police officer or elected official being bullied. Only peers, those of similar age or status, of the bullied can stop or prevent such behavior.

You have much more power than you think. You may be able to stop it by simply telling the bully to knock it off. Especially if two or more of you do it together. It is much more difficult for a bully to stand up to a group than an individual. If that doesn't work, you may have to speak to a teacher or other adult.

Wearing a t-shirt or hanging a poster that says "Stop Bullying" won't do it. Nor will money. Talking about it does nothing.

If you are bullied, you need to ask for help from one or more of your friends. If a friend asks for help, then help them. Better yet, don't make them ask for help.

You have seen professional athletes stick up for their communities and help those in need. Well, the bullied are in need of your support.

You have more power than you think to turn your school into a place that fosters empathy and inclusion! If you and your friends wanted to stop bullying in our communities, it it is up to you. You can end bullying tomorrow by working together and demonstrating a little courage.

II

Manners & Stuff

8

Thanks a Million!

Writing a hand written thank you note is a lost art. The convenience of digital communications, the perceived lack of time and change in social norms and manners have all contributed to the scarcity of the written thank you note. But don't fool yourself; smart, successful people value manners and king of manners is the thank you note. So let's go through a few pieces of etiquette:

When to write a thank you

- When you receive a gift – birthday, Christmas, confirmation, graduation, etc.
- When someone does something nice for you or goes above and beyond what is asked of them
- After a job interview – want to stick out from other candidates, send a note
- When you had dinner or stayed overnight at someone's home.
- And when someone throws a party or event for you.

Anytime someone does something extraordinary after which simply saying "thank you" doesn't seem like enough – it's time to write a thank you. Even if you thank them, there's never a wrong time to write a note.

Thank you parameters

Write the note as soon as possible. Send it within two weeks of the event or receiving the gift. But if time gets away from you, send it later.

Send it by mail. This is one time it's worth it to splurge on a stamp! Email or text thank yous are convenient, but they do not have the impact of the handwritten note. Sending a thank you note through the mail shows effort. It shows that you took the time to write a note, address the envelope, and buy a stamp. It makes your thank you much more sincere.

Use real stationery or thank you notes. Make it easy on yourself and invest in some nice looking stationery or note cards. That way you'll always have the necessary items to write the note. You don't need thank you notes. You can buy paper that is versatile enough for other purposes.

How to Write a Thank You Note

The format of a written thank you is actually very simple. You can get by with writing very little as long as you do it well. Three or four short paragraphs is all it takes to formulate a nice thank you note.

Begin by thanking the giver for the gift or experience. This can be a simple: "Thank you very much for _____." If the gift was money, you can say something like "thank you for thinking of me."

Then tell the giver how you plan to use a gift or what you enjoyed about the experience. This is especially true for a monetary gift; tell the giver what you plan to spend it on or what you're saving for.

When appropriate, you can add some news about your life. If you're writing a thank you note for a job interview, you don't want to tell them how you recently caught a two-foot bass. But if you receive a gift from grandparents, give a brief sketch about what you've been up to recently.

Finally, you can end by referencing the past or looking forward to the future. "It was great to see you at Christmas," and/or "I hope we all can get together again next year," work fine for this. If the person sent the gift in the mail, and you see them infrequently, simply write, "I hope to see you soon."

Repeat your thanks. "Thank you again for the gift," makes the perfect last line.

Nothing shows your appreciation like a written note. If you want to stand out, <u>write</u> a thank you note.

9

Takin' Care of Business

There are intricate rules of decorum that govern the men's room. Once you know them, you'll find that many men don't know or follow them – but you'll appreciate those who do..

Decisions, Decisions!

If you're the first one there, choose the urinal furthest from the door. If you're second in, choose the one on the opposite end. If you're third in, choose the middle. Try to leave at least one urinal gap between users.

Of course, sometimes the only urinal available is right next to another person. You have a decision to make, you can either prepare for an awkward encounter in which you try to avoid getting too close to the guy next to you, or you can wait your turn rather than feel like you're invading another guy's space. The partitions between urinals was the greatest invention ever.

Keep Both Hands on the Wheel

Two-handed is the professional industry standard. One-handed will be allowed.

Eye Straight Ahead & Zip it!

The men's room is not the place to meet new friends because

when you meet someone, what do you usually do? Shake hands – and who wants to shake hands at the urinal?!

If you are really compelled to introduce yourself, do your job, wash your hands and meet the guy outside the restroom!

Don't strike up a conversation or tell your latest joke. Don't be the guy who walks into the bathroom and tries to strike up a conversation. It's just not the time or the place.

You will be met with a bunch of guys doing what you should be doing – staring straight ahead while they relieve themselves! Some bathrooms even have newspaper articles or pictures to look at in front of you. There are reasons for this.

Please no peeking! It's a good way to get yourself decked. Keep your eyes on your business or on the wall, never ever talk to a guy or glance at him. Get it done and get out. When standing at the sink, it's okay to look at yourself in the mirror, but absolutely never should peeking at your neighbor be allowed. Period.

Technique is Everything

Keep your feet together or you risk splash from the next guy's urinal hitting you in the foot. (I wouldn't wear flip flops in to the men's room if at all possible for the same reason!) You should not be staking out more turf here.

Aim! If you shoot straight ahead, you might just splash yourself. Shoot at the drain or just above. Some fancy urinals even have targets to keep you focused. That way to don't sprinkle everything in sight!

Remember when you were young? "If you sprinkle when your tinkle, please be neat and wipe the seat..." Don't leave leftovers for the next person. Wiping up another guy's dribbles ain't happening and soon all the toilets are out of commission for future users!

Save the name writing for the snow and don't try to hit all the drain holes! This isn't a game, just aim down and let it fly.

And flush the damn toilet!

Liquids Only Please

No gum, sunflower seeds or big green loogies in the urinal. No one should have to look at that or clean it out of there. Show some class!

Know "Man Code"!

There is a code for "I'm in this stall and you're not invited!" – a cough or a clearing of the throat usually works fine. As soon as you hear the door open, you need to make your presence known.

No Musical Accompaniment

Please no singing, humming or whistling. You can practice your musicianship later.

Leave Your Phone Alone

Phone have cameras and cameras in bathrooms are not appropriate. No texts, no tweets, no Snaps, no phones! This is not the place for multitasking!

No Loitering!

The men's room is more of a drive through than a sit down meal. Guys hanging in the bathroom is creepy. Do your thing and move on. It's annoying when someone is done but still stands there, zipping, belting, tucking and dithering, occupying the urinal space without actually using it. You can zip on the way to the sink. The men's room is not the place to linger.

10

Hold That Door!

Holding a door for a woman is a chivalrous tradition. Chivalry includes the noble qualities of a knight including gallantry, courtesy and honor. Our culture has changed and so has this tradition. It's now more traditional to hold a door for anyone, male or female.

Don't Think!

The process of holding the door for someone is very simple and straightforward. It seems that the more one thinks about it, the more difficult it can be. Be natural and use common sense.

If you get to the door before someone, opening the door is simple. Just open the door and hold it. When you arrive at the door at the same time another person for whom you want to open the door, just grab the door handle and open. If the person gets there before you, it might make more sense to just forget it.

In or out?

If a door opens inward, you should go through the door before the other person in order to hold it for them. Try to avoid the situation where you're standing in the doorway holding the door open with your back. If the door swings out, just pull the door open and step aside allowing the person to pass before you.

Let me get that!

If you see an older person, a person with an obvious physical impairment or someone who has their hands full, it's best to let them know that you have the door and encourage them to wait for just a moment.

If you are entering a building where there is an exterior door, an entryway airlock area, and then an interior door, open the exterior door but not the second unless the person actually needs help with the second (physical impairment or with hands full). In that case, allow the person to step inside the airlock and then let them know you will get the second door as well.

You don't have to be the doorman

Just because you hold the door for one person does not mean you have to be a door man. After the person you're holding the door for has walked through the door, follow them through. Of course, this doesn't mean you should just let a door slam shut in somebody's face. As you pass through the door, look behind you to see if anybody is following close behind and hold the door open long enough for them to take control of the door.

37

Don't be offended if someone wants to open the door for themselves; let them. Move on and don't take it personally. It's unfortunate that some people cannot deal with the courtesy extended to them.

Holding doors is an act of common courtesy that you can show to any person, man or woman. If someone opens a door for you, always smile and say, "Thank you!"

11

What's With All the Spoons?

Have you ever sat down at the dinner table and wondered why all the forks? Or spoons? Or knives? If so, you're not alone. Most people don't have many opportunities to learn or practice formal table manners often enough to be confident that they're using the silverware correctly.

It's not as difficult as you might think. Like anything, you develop confidence by actually doing it. Knowing which fork to use for each course begins to feel natural, and eventually you won't have to think about what to do next.

Whether you are trying to make a good impression on a love interest or a prospective employer, knowing which utensils to use at a formal dinner is essential. You can show your knowledge of proper etiquette whether you're at an elegant dinner party or eating at a 5-star restaurant.

Follow Your Host's Lead

If you are not certain about which fork to use, follow the lead of the host (the person whose home you're at or who is buying dinner at the restaurant). Even if he or she uses the wrong fork, you'll show your respect by doing the same thing. Just don't bring attention to yourself or embarrass the host.

Start on the Outside and Work Your Way In

Utensils are generally placed so you can follow them in order from the one farthest from the plate and work your way inward. Forks are on the left, with the salad fork first, and then the dinner fork beside the plate. On the right side of the plate, you will find the knife, appetizer or salad knife, spoon, soup spoon, and oyster fork. The knife blades should be positioned with the cutting sides closest to the plate. The fork and knife closest to the plate are for eating your main course.

The dessert fork or spoon in most cases will be placed parallel or diagonal to the edge of the table near the top of your plate. In some cases, it may be set on the empty dessert plate. Not all formal place settings will have all the flatware mentioned; you will only find what you will need for the courses.

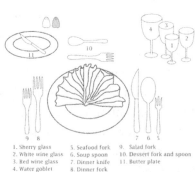

The Formal Table Setting

1. Sherry glass	5. Seafood fork	9. Salad fork
2. White wine glass	6. Soup spoon	10. Dessert fork and spoon
3. Red wine glass	7. Dinner knife	11. Butter plate
4. Water goblet	8. Dinner fork	

Proper Eating Techniques

During a formal dinner, you should use the correct utensil and follow the proper method of eating with these utensils as well. The American technique to cut meat is to place the fork in your non-dominant hand and place the knife in your dominant hand (righties use right hand, lefties use left hand) to cut the meat. Then put down the knife and switch the fork to your more coordinated hand to lift the bite-sized pieces to your mouth.

The British etiquette for cutting and eating meat is to not switch the fork, but to lift the meat to your mouth with the fork with your non-dominant hand which saves you the step of switching hands each time you need to cut the meat.

Use the round or larger oval spoon to eat soup. You should not lift or tilt the bowl. Using your soup spoon, scoop the soup away from you starting at the center of the bowl. Bring the spoon to your mouth and tilt it while sipping soup from the edge. You should never make a slurping noise when eating soup and you shouldn't lift the bowl to drink the last few drops that you can't scoop with the spoon.

Don't use your fork to eat bread. Tear off bite-sized pieces and butter them one or two bites at a time. It is awkward and messy to butter an entire slice of bread.

Additional Tips

Each of the utensils are tools and have a specific purpose. Just as you use a hammer for a specific purpose, so too with utensils at a formal dinner. Learn the function of each utensil and you won't have any problems.

While it may be fine to eat chicken or pork chops with your hands at the family reunion, that isn't the case at formal dinners. You should always use your fork.

You should place your utensils on your plate before picking up a glass or cup to drink any beverage. After you use each utensil, rest it on the edge of your plate; don't put it back on the table. When you are done eating, place your utensils at four o'clock on your plate.

Don't worry about screwing up. People likely won't notice as long as you don't call it to their attention. You may find that you know as much or more about formal dinner etiquette than many others at the table. But you should avoid calling others out on improper etiquette because that shows poor manners, certainly worse than using the wrong fork.

Don't turn down that invitation to a formal dinner because you're intimidated. Take some time to learn these skills and enjoy that great meal!

12

Don't Be Tardy to the Party!

Do you know someone who is late for everything? No matter the event, you can count on this person to be late. I'll bet you also know someone who is always punctual. They are NEVER late. In fact they are always early.

Punctuality (always being on time) or tardiness are key ways we brand ourselves. Just like the people you thought of when you read the paragraph above.

When you are late for appointments, you will have wasted one of people's most valuable assets, their time. They may view you as rude, irresponsible and disrespectful. Ask yourself if this how I want to brand myself?

Being on time demonstrates that you are diligent and dependable. It indicates that you can be trusted to keep your commitments and shows that you respect other people's time as much as your own.

Not only should you make every effort to be on time for business-related appointments, but you should also do your utmost to be on time for personal commitments. Valuing your friend's time and earning their respect is an important part of your individual reputation.

Why arrive early

It's good to give yourself a little cushion in case something delays you. When you show up at the exact time of your appointment you have no room for error.

If you arrive just under the wire, you come rushing through the door stressed and unorganized. Arriving a few minutes early allows you to be relaxed and prepared for the appointment.

You won't have to make up an excuse for being late when you arrive a few minutes early. Excuses are like noses, everyone has one. Don't be the guy with all the excuses.

When your best plan fails

Sometimes stuff happens and it won't always be possible to be on time. If you are going to be late for an appointment, call as soon as you are able. This allows others to plan their schedules accordingly. Cell phones and other technology make this an easy thing to do.

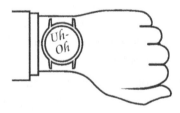

Why punctuality matters

What is your brand? Are you someone who shows respect for others' time? Are you trustworthy? Are you a reliable person?

Take pride in being a person who is always on time and

prepared for your appointments. Remember, there is no down-side in showing up early, but there is significant downside to showing up late.

When you are on time you enhance your brand. When you are late, you devalue your brand. Being on time is a choice.

III

Your Body & Stuff

13

Think Before You Ink

Turn on a televised sporting event and you see athletes with tattoos all over themselves. It doesn't matter whether you're watching NBA, NFL, MLB or college sports, you will almost certainly see at least one athlete with a visible tattoo.

That has almost certainly caused younger athletes to aspire to having a tattoo. Should you have a tattoo? How many? What's the difference between you and that professional athlete when it comes to tattoos?

The tattoo obsession may hinder young people's ability to find work and disqualify many from career opportunities. While it is a trend that is fueled by professional athletes, music artists and celebrities, there is a difference between you and them.

Now that's not to say, a well-designed, thought-out and executed tattoo isn't just fine. However, before you run out and get one, sit down and think about it - because it's permanent. Getting a tattoo at the spur-of-the-moment is the one of the worst things you can do.

Always remember that image is incredibly important and you only have roughly 10-seconds to make a good impression. My best advice: don't want to get a tattoo anywhere you can't cover with reasonable clothing. The tattoo needs to be covered-up if necessary. That means do not get one on neck, face, or hands, period.

Many companies have policies on visible tattoos that may prevent a person from being hired or placed in certain positions. They have become one of the most common employment barriers facing young job seekers. We can argue whether that's fair or not, but the reality is that body art or excessive tattoos can affect your employment options.

Permanent reminder of a temporary feeling –Jimmy Buffett

The FDA estimated that as many as 45 million Americans have tattoos. The report based the number on the finding by a Harris Interactive poll that found 16 percent of adults and 36 percent of people age 25 to 29 had at least one tattoo. A recent poll also found that 17 percent of tattooed Americans regretted it. A tattoo that cost several hundred dollars could require several thousand dollars and many laser sessions to remove.

Tattoos are not cheap! In February 2020, the average cost for a small tattoo like a heart or cross is $50 to $250. For a medium-sized tattoo like a tribal or portrait, expect to spend between $150 and $450. Hiring a tattoo artist typically costs $120 to $150 per hour, and prices depend on how long it takes.

Many adults regret things that they have done in their teen years. Many experts agree that the biggest mistakes of a person's life often happen between the ages of 16 and 24. If young men and women would simply take the time to think beyond their immediate desire and consider the long-term effect of their decisions, they may find that the ink isn't worth the price.

It's my body!

The most common argument in support of tattoos art is that it's your body and it's your way of demonstrating self-expression. While that is absolutely true, the question is how much are you willing to make a fashion statement or personal expression if it may also limit your capacity to make a living? At what cost are you willing to use our body as a platform to make a statement?

Think before you ink!

Taking the time to think before making a decision that could be permanent is simply a wise thing to do.

14

By the Hair on My Chinny Chin Chin

Your voice may be cracking a bit. You might notice your facial hair starting to come in. You'll also start seeing hair grow in under your armpits, around your groin, on your belly, and on your chest (maybe even on your back though that is usually reserved for later!). All the extra hair is the result of hormones called androgens, which kick in at puberty.

And while it's probably not time to grow a mustache (or beard) - mainly because you can't, it may be time to consider shaving your face.

If you shave those little strands of hair for a while, it won't be long and you can grow facial hair. You don't look any older when you grow fifteen light hairs under your nose. There's no need to show everyone that you cannot grow a decent stand of facial hair.

You should start shaving when you decide that you have enough hair growth on your face to actually shave off. You'll notice darker hairs forming on your chin and around your upper lip.

In the meantime, here are some tips on how to shave your

facial hair:

You need to find a razor that is safe and that works well for you.

Electric or Manual?

Electric razors are convenient but, generally, do not shave as close as the disposable razors. Some have flexible heads to conform to the contours of your face. Some electric razors dispense lubricants that help soften and protect your skin. An electric razor can still irritate your skin. It can take time to find one that's right for you.

Disposable razors require some type of shaving cream or gel to apply to your face before shaving to lubricate your face and reduce the risk of cutting your skin. There are many creams and gels to choose from.

The best time to shave is after taking a warm bath or shower to make your skin hydrated and soft. Splash warm water on your face applying shaving cream or gel. Massage your face and neck with it to help putting cream under the whiskers and lift them up. This will make it easier for the razor to make contact because the hairs will stick out.

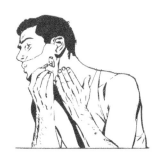

Lather up!

Apply shaving cream or gel which produces lather and helps protect the skin as the razor cuts the hair.

Shave with the grain of your hair. Whiskers on the face usually grow down, so shaving downward on the face removes most of the hair. Shaving against the grain can cause rashes or red bumps.

Take your time and don't push down too hard with the razor. Use soft, short strokes on your jaw and chin.

A styptic pencil can be used to stop bleeding if you nick yourself. To use: dip the white pencil in water and then apply it to the nick.

You should change razors or blades frequently although when you first start shaving, your blade won't dull as soon as it will when your hair is thicker and more course. A dull blade can irritate your skin and is more likely to cut your face.

When you're done, wash your face with soap and water. Then follow up your shave with a face lotion to prevent your skin from drying out.

Unless you have very thick facial hair, you don't have to shave every day when you first start shaving. Try to shave the darker hairs that are starting to come in, and wait for the full-face shave. There will be plenty of time for daily shaving later!

15

Your Body - The Owners Manual

When you're 13 years old, you think you're bulletproof. You think you can do anything, eat anything, subject your body to anything and there will not be any consequences. And there aren't any - immediately.

When you're 40 years old, you start to wish you'd have taken better care of yourself. When you're 50 years old your really wish you'd have taken better care of yourself. And when you're 60+ years old... Well, you know...

Your body is your temple. Treat it well. Here are three things you can do to have fewer regrets later in life.

Don't eat too much junk food

Notice I did not say don't eat ANY junk food. I did that because it is virtually impossible to avoid it completely. Just try to minimize it.

Food is fuel. You will get performance from your body equal to the fuel you feed it!

Too much sugar and you'll crash. Candy diets and processed food binges aren't part of a healthy lifestyle. Soda, chips, pizza and sugar are all poisonous to your system. You can be a "workout warrior", but your body can only use the materials you provide to get bigger, faster, stronger.

Give your body the fuel it needs to become what you want to be!

Get some sleep!

Lack of sleep is not a trophy. Bragging about only getting three hours of sleep last night is not something to be proud of. What it shows is a severe lack of balance. Life is a marathon, not a sprint.

Most adults need between six and eight hours of sleep per day. Adolescents need at least seven and a half and would do much better with eight or more. Why? Because your body is growing – and fast!

You may find yourself more tired some days. It only means your body is changing and it requires sleep to do so efficiently.

All sleep is not equal. That sleep that comes before 10:00 pm is best. Sleeping in until noon if you go to bed at 4 am is not the same as going to bed at 10 pm and awaking at 6 am.

Move!

Physical activity is crucial to personal wellness. No matter how busy you get, or how hectic things are, you always have to make time to take care of your physical body. Exercise is key. If you don't, you'll pay for it later.

You don't need an organized workout to fulfill this need. Just get off the couch and move. Take the dog for a walk. Mow the lawn (with a push mower!). Go out and play catch with a friend.

If you are playing an active sport, you have this covered. But don't quit moving in the off season.

You can be who you want to be. Your body is a reflection of who you are, your habits, how you treat yourself, everything. Cut out the bad stuff.

IV

Skills & Stuff

16

Tools of the Trade

I never had decent tools until I was forty years old. I had a hand-me-down toolbox full of orphaned tools that I had accumulated over the years. Nothing matched. My 1/2" socket was from a different set than my 3/4" socket. My straight screwdriver was different than my Phillips screwdriver. Every job that required tools was frustrating because it seemed like I never had the right tool or because my tools were cheap, they'd break.

So when I got a gift certificate for Lowe's, I decided I was going to use it to finally upgrade my tools. I bought some high quality tools. Since then, every home repair or handyman task is so much easier. I actually enjoy some of them!

Parents and grandparents always struggle to find a good gift for a young man. Young men aren't very good at offering suggestions other than the latest video game or tech gadget, both of which are likely to be obsolete within a year.

Tools are a timeless gift or purchase that can be used again and again either to assist someone or to fix something for yourself. Maybe your love interest needs help assembling some furniture. What a great way to impress that important someone in your life - breaking out a set of quality tools to help her with the job!

Owning a well equipped toolbox is something that many young men leave to their dads. Then when you have a project, you have to either borrow tools or enlist help. A man should be self-reliant. He should have the tools and know-how to tackle basic projects around the house.

Toolbox

Keeping your collection of drivers, screws, and bolts in an easy-to-haul toolbox keeps things organized and handy. Toolboxes come in a variety of shapes, sizes, materials and functions. Plan ahead and get one that will serve you today and as your tool collection grows.

Hammer

A 16-ounce claw hammer is versatile and works well for driving nails into walls, assembling or just general handyman tasks. The curved claw is useful for pulling out the nails that inevitably get bent.

Cordless drill & bits

A good cordless drill is a must in any toolbox. A drill's power is measured by the voltage of its battery. But when you increase voltage, you increase weight. For example, a 12 volt drill is a nice balance of power and light weight for drilling holes or driving screw. It's enough power to tackle most tasks around the house but isn't too heavy. You want a drill that has multiple speeds and is reversible. I recommend springing for the spare battery.

Pliers

A staple of every toolbox, pliers can be used to straighten bent power-cord plugs, replace old shower heads, slice wiring, and get a good grip on just about anything. A pair of needle nose pliers will help get into those narrow spots. You can purchase them as a set.

Locking pliers

Pliers that can lock in place can be used as pliers, a pipe wrench, an adjustable wrench, wire cutters, a ratchet, or a clamp. They come in handy when you need an extra hand.

Screwdrivers

Screwdrivers are versatile tools that can be used to tighten cabinet hardware, install light switches, and crack open the lids on metal paint cans. They can be purchased with interchangeable heads or in multi-screwdrivers sets. A ten-piece set would include all the common slotted and Phillips-head sizes, as well as stubby versions to get into tight spots.

Tape measure

"Measure twice and cut once" is the old adage. A good measuring tape makes it easy to measure twice. You will measure anything from the wall area for a paint project to the thickness of lumber at the home center—where you'll learn that a 2x4 is not exactly 2 by 4 inches.

Adjustable wrench

The versatility of the adjustable wrench is hard to beat. This is your one tool to tighten and assemble all manner of swing sets and appliances as well as plumbing fixtures. A 6- and 10-inch wrench equips you for almost any job.

Utility knife

When you need to open boxes, sharpen pencils, or shave wood, the utility knife is your tool. The deluxe model has a comfortable rubber-covered handle and built-in blade storage.

Handsaw

The symbol of a craftsman, a handsaw is used to cut the wood for your project. It can also be used to trim branches off a tree.

Level

If you don't want your pictures hanging crooked or you want your cabinets to be level, the level is a must-have tool. A sturdy metal one is less prone to dings than a plastic one and will be in your toolbox for a long time.

Duct Tape

If it can't be fixed with duct tape, it cannot be fixed! Duct tape adheres to just about anything and has a thick, woven backing. Use it to repair torn tarps, broken buckets, and just about everything else.

Flashlight

A rechargeable work light that you leave plugged in will relieve you from the frustration of looking for fresh batteries every time you need portable light. The new LED generation of flashlights are extra bright and have extended battery life.

Safety glasses

A good quality set of safety glasses not only protects your eyes, but fit well and are scratch resistant. If they don't come with a case, grab a single sock from the sock drawer to put them in to prevent scratches. If you value your eyes, you need to wear these.

Work gloves

You might want a pair of full-finger gloves and a pair of the kind that leaves the fingertips exposed. Either way, a quality pair of gloves will last a long time.

Quality tools are not cheap - but they are worth the money. They will serve the owner for a lifetime if they are cared for and not abused. Many quality tools have a lifetime warranty. Resist the temptation to go to Wal-mart and buy a prepackaged box of tools for $30. Quality tools are an investment that return to you every time you use them.

Unless you have deep pockets, you need to prioritize and acquire your tools one at a time. Ask for specific tools as gifts.

Before long, your toolbox will start to grow heavy!

17

Jump At The Chance

I was pretty lucky when I went off to college. My parents bought me a pretty dependable car. It was an orange and white 1978 Ford Pinto. It wasn't a muscle car but it was reliable, got good fuel economy and I had upgraded the stereo!

I realized how fortunate I was when I got to school and saw what some of the other students were driving - if they had a car at all. Some of these vehicles barely qualified as transportation!

When the cold Omaha winter hit, some of my friends saw for the first time what cold weather does to a vehicle's starting ability. The Omaha winter exposed the weak batteries!

My parents had equipped me with a set of jumper cables. They knew an Omaha winter wasn't much milder than a South Dakota winter. When cars wouldn't start, word got out that I had these magical cables and I became a popular guy. Not only did I have jumper cables, I actually knew how to use them!

Knowing how to jump start a car is a fundamental skill for any driver. It is an especially important skill to know if you drive a less than reliable car or live in an area where you experience severe winters.

Like I found out, even if you drive a reliable vehicle, you probably have friends or know people who don't. In that case, it's a great opportunity to help someone in need!

The tools needed to jump start a car are very simple – a good set of jumper cables. Some people believe that longer cables make the task easier.

While it's true you gain flexibility in positioning your vehicles, that convenience is offset by the fact that longer cables lose some power the longer they are. Heavy cabled jumper cables will carry more power and will be helpful!

Safety First

There are safety risks to consider before performing a jump start. First, make sure that there are no children in the area as you maneuver the vehicles for connections. You'll also want to ensure children are not present when you make connections.

It's not a bad idea to check your vehicle's owners manual to determine if there are any special steps required to successfully jump your vehicle.

When you handle jumper cables, you should be aware that that the cables will be transmitting electric current and you must be careful not to receive a shock. Do not let cable ends touch each other or you risk shock or damage to the vehicles' batteries.

Finally, you should wear eye protection. It's a good idea to store protective glasses with your jumper cables so they are available. Sparks can fly when the connections are made.

Prepare for the Jump

You will need to park the cars so that the cables are long enough to reach the batteries of both vehicles. Often, it's easiest to park them facing each other so that there is enough room to get between them – about 15-20 inches apart. Do not allow them to touch!

Put automatic vehicles in park or manual transmission in neutral. Set the parking brake so neither car moves.

Ensure that both vehicles are turned off. Then open the hoods on both vehicles and find the batteries. Some vehicles will have a jump point with the battery located elsewhere. The terminals on either a battery or a jump point will be covered in red or black, with a + or − sign on top.

Be certain you can identify which is positive, and which is negative. A wrong connection can be dangerous and can ruin your batteries. This distinction is crucial to the success of your jump. If the battery terminals are dirty, wipe them off with a rag or wire brush.

Connect the Vehicles

You should attach the red, positive cable clamp to the positive (+) battery terminal of the dead battery. Make sure you have a solid connection to the battery terminal. This may require some initial wiggling of the clamps

Then attach the red, positive cable clamp on the other side of the jumper cables to the functioning vehicle's positive (+) battery terminal. Again you must ensure a solid connection.

Next, you can connect the black, negative cable clamp to the working battery's negative (−) battery terminal.

Do not connect the black, negative cable clamp to the dead battery. Instead, attach that clamp to an unpainted, metal part of the car such as a shiny, clean nut on the engine block. This will help ensure a safe jump.

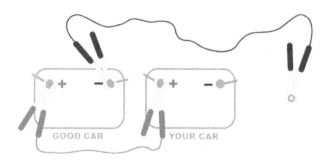

Jump Start Vehicle

Start the vehicle with the charged battery. Allow it to run for 2–3 minutes or longer depending on the status of the dead battery. If the battery is older and/or it has a very low charge, you may have to wait longer.

Try starting the dead car. If the car doesn't start, allow the working vehicle to charge the battery for some additional time before attempting again (the longer, the better). In some instances, slightly revving the engine of the working car while charging the dead battery may help.

When the dead car is started, disconnect the jumper cables, starting with the black, negative cable clamps. Do not let the clamps touch each other while any part of the cables is still attached to a car.

The driver of the vehicle with the dead battery should keep the vehicle running for awhile or take a short drive. This will allow the battery to build up a charge. This driving allows the vehicle's alternator to charge the battery and ensures that the vehicle does not die again once it is turned it off.

If Vehicle Won't Start

If the jump fails to start your car after a few short attempts, or if the car starts but then dies again, you have some other issues

73

you need to address. Most batteries are rated to last 4-6 years. If your battery is old, you may need to replace it.

If the battery should be working well, you should consider other possible problems with other components, fuses, battery corrosion, faulty alternator, ignition switch or starter connection.

Even if your get the vehicle started, it's a good idea to try to determine why the battery was dead. Common causes include: leaving headlights, interior lights, flashers, or the radio on when the car isn't running; using the air conditioner when the car is not running; not starting a car for long periods of time (e.g., while it's in storage); lack of battery maintenance (e.g., not keeping terminals clean).

18

Rockin' the Junior High Dance

I started my informal career as a DJ when I was a sophomore in high school. A friend and I combined our stereo equipment, rented the City Hall, convinced our parents to chaperone (only way we could get the use of City Hall) and played the hits of the day.

We charged one dollar per head at the door and used that money to upgrade our equipment several times. By the time we were seniors, we had pretty good equipment. We had also figured our how to record the songs on cassette tape (with crossover fading!) so we could partake in the boogieing too!

Since that time, I have served as DJ for many, many dances and events. My equipment has been upgraded considerably. Each year I am "hired" to DJ the local middle school dance (because I'm cheap/free!). Each year I am reminded how challenging a dance can be for middle school students.

There aren't that many opportunities to attend dances for middle school (or even high school) students. You want to make the best of those moments. Here are a few tips to help you do just that.

Follow the theme

Most school dances have a theme or are held to celebrate a holiday, special event or a season, such as Valentine's Day, homecoming, or spring. Understanding what the theme of the dance is all about will help you be more prepared for the big event. For example, if it's a Halloween Dance, wear a costume!

Bring some cash

Most dance sponsors charge a nominal fee to pay for dance expenses and/or raise some funds. A fee of approximately $10 per student is common. Sometimes tickets may be sold a week or two before, or sold at the door the night of the dance. If you have to buy a ticket before the dance, make sure you allow plenty of time. Admission may or may not usually cover refreshments. Bring a little extra cash so you can buy that dance partner a bottle of water after shaking on the floor!

Who else will be rockin'?

Your middle school dance may be open to the entire school, or it might be specific to one grade. These are details you can easily learn at school or by asking friends. Small schools may invite students from a neighboring school to the dance in order to share costs and give kids a chance to make new friends and mingle with kids from other schools.

What to wear

You may be anxious about what to wear to the school dance. High school dances may be semi-formal, formal or casual. For semi-formal and formal events, a suit or a shirt and tie often works for guys.

Most middle school dances are casual and are the easiest to dress for: jeans and a nice shirt are sure to satisfy the dress code. Try to step up from your favorite t-shirt and hoodie. Girls will be impressed with a polo or button down shirt. Remember, you look older and more mature when you dress up a bit.

Rockin' the dance floor

Your first middle school dance is often the first time you'll be dancing with a huge group of people (except when you danced with Grandma at Aunt Becky's wedding dance). Sometimes dancing in front of peers can be stressful.

It gets easier if you just get out on the floor and shake! You don't have to dance with a specific person. If you start dancing, all the girls will want to dance with you – and they will! You'll have way more fun on the dance floor than you will leaning up against the wall.

You can expect simple, high-energy songs with an occasional slow song. If you're not sure, on the high-energy songs, it's often best to just get out on the floor and dance like your friends dance.

Slow songs will require a dance partner, which may be a little stressful the first time through. Just ask "Want to dance with me?"

If the other person accepts your offer to dance, choose whatever open spot on the floor is available. Girls should place their arms around your shoulders or hang their arms around your neck. You should place hands on your dance partner's waist or around their back.

If you are not sure how close you should be with your dance partner, just ask them. "Is this okay?" will be fine and can help save you some embarrassment. Look down at where your partner's feet are and just be sure you don't step on their feet (but be sure not to look down the whole time).

Don't ask the DJ to play a song unless you're going to dance to it. He/she has a list of songs from people who will dance.

Whether you take to the floor or not, have fun. Dances are social events so mix it up with your friends and classmates.

19

All Joking Aside

Why would you want to be good at joke-telling? Let's face it, people who make those around them laugh are more fun! Telling a joke is actually a great way to show off your stature and confidence.

Whatever motivates you, just make sure you have some jokes to tell. Learning any new skill requires practice. With practice though, virtually anyone can learn to be a joke teller.

What makes a joke funny

Take some time to listen to master joke-tellers. Get on YouTube and watch them as you listen. Watch their facial expressions, their eyes, their body language and hand gestures.

What makes their jokes so funny? Is it their accents, details, embellishments? Listen to their voice and how they tell their joke. How does their voice change? Do they leave open pauses in their deliveries?

Two people can tell the same joke and get completely different reactions. It's all about HOW they tell the joke.

You need good jokes!

It doesn't matter how good your delivery is, if the joke is no good, people won't laugh. Find a good joke to practice. The are many good sites online or you can buy a joke book. You may be drawn to a particular genre of joke (dog jokes, little Johnny jokes, North Dakota jokes, etc.). That's a great place to start.

Once you have identified a joke you like, start adding details to it. If there is a part of it you find distracting, discard or change it. Once you feel satisfied with the joke's components, write it down and start practicing.

Practice, practice, practice

Start practicing your joke in the shower or while you are alone playing video games. Record yourself and play it back. Can you tell the joke without lots of weird pauses, ums, and ahs? It's no different than anything else – to be good at it, you must practice.

The fastest way to ruin a joke is to read it instead of telling it. You can always tell when someone is reading a joke of performing it if they say "he replied" or "she responded." People don't tell jokes like that!

Keep it simple

Jokes that require accents (southern drawl, Norwegian accent, etc.) are more difficult. Accents take a great deal of practice to master. Jokes with many intricate details can be more challenging. Save them until you're better at telling jokes.

Embellish!

The best joke tellers include interesting detail. If you mention a car in your joke, try giving it some personality. Is it a lime Ford F-150? Use people's names. Make your audience feel like they know the characters. The more details you include, the more your audience can believe that it is a personal story. Add names of bars, restaurants or intersections.

Consider your audience

The jokes that bust your buddies up may not have the same effect on Grandma. Save the F-bombs. Most people laugh at that not because it's funny but because it's a nervous reaction to an uncomfortable situation.

Think about whether your jokes are offensive to your audience before you tell them. You're better off not telling a joke than you are telling the wrong one!

Few more tips

- If everybody has heard the joke, change the major details, the delivery or the ending to restore the element of surprise back to a time-worn joke.
- Frame the story as your own. If your friends think you are telling them a serious story, the punch line can be a big surprise.
- Keep your joke short – but not too short. Keep it around a minute.
- Add some sound effects. A joke is a story and the story is better with sounds.

Here are a few of my favorite animal jokes. Feel free to use them!

A blind man with a seeing eye dog at his side walks into a

grocery store. The man walks to the middle of the store, picks up the dog by the tail, and starts swinging the dog around in circles over his head.

The store manager, who has seen all this, thinks this is quite strange. So, he decides to find out what's going on. The store manager approaches the blind man swinging the dog and says, "Pardon me. May I help you with something."

The blind man says, "No thanks. I'm just looking around."

* * *

A man went to visit a friend and was amazed to find him playing chess with his dog. He watched the game in astonishment for a while. "I can hardly believe my eyes!" he exclaimed. "That's the smartest dog I've ever seen."

"Nah, he's not so smart," the friend replied. "I've beaten him three games out of five."

* * *

A duck walks into a bar and asks the bartender if he has any grapes. The bartender replies that he doesn't have any grapes.

The next day the duck walks into the same bar and again asks the bartender if he has any grapes, and again the bartender tells him that he doesn't.

This goes on for a week, until the frustrated bartender warns the duck that if he asks that stupid question one more time, he's going to staple the duck's bill closed.

The next day the duck walks into the bar and asks the bartender, "Do you have any staples?"

The bartender says, "No." So the duck says, "Good. In that

case, do you have any grapes?"

* * *

I went to the cinema the other day and in the front row was an old man and with him was his dog. It was a sad funny kind of film, you know the type. In the sad part, the dog cried his eyes out, and in the funny part, the dog laughed its head off. This happened all the way through the film. After the film had ended, I decided to go and speak to the man.

"That's the most amazing thing I've seen," I said. "That dog really seemed to enjoy the film."

The man turned to me and said, "Yeah, it is. He hated the book."

20

What's Burning? - How to Cook a Signature Dish

I love to cook. I love to eat!. These two activities compliment each other well.

I have always enjoyed hosting friends and family and so my love of cooking fits right into that. Food has always been a centerpiece of our gatherings.

When I was younger, my culinary skills were limited. That, however, did not slow me down. I enjoyed cooking cheeseburgers at the baptism or 4th of July gatherings. Our guests seemed to enjoy eating them as well.

As I got more experience (grew older), I started experimenting with other foods. Most of that was on the grill but I eventually expanded my horizons beyond that outdoor burner.

We built a wood-fired oven in our backyard some time ago. I loved the idea of making wood-fired pizza at home.

It took me two years to make a pizza that I wasn't embarrassed to serve and almost five years to make one that I was proud of. It was that thin, crispy pizza crust that was so elusive. Now I'll put my pizza up against anyone's!

My signature pizza dish is the wood-fired margherita pizza; simple fresh tomato sauce, fresh mozzarella cheese and fresh basil combo on a thin, crisp crust is the original pizza from Naples, Italy.

A signature dish is a recipe that identifies an individual chef. If you are a famous chef, it should be unique and allow an informed gastronome to name the chef in a blind tasting. If you're a young man, it should mean that anyone who knows you well will drop what they are doing and come eat when they hear you are cooking your signature dish.

You do not have to know how to cook a lot of foods to be a good cook. You need to know how to make a few. If you learn to make a main dish, you will soon want to learn to make side dishes that go with it. Then you will be able to prepare an entire meal and, I promise, you will be regarded as a great cook!

You can buy virtually any food frozen and ready to pop into the microwave. Some of these foods are good. Some are edible. Some should not be eaten. FROZEN FOOD CANNOT BE A SIGNATURE DISH.

It's also that dish that you feel confident preparing and serving no matter what! You know its nuances, you know how it should taste, you know that it will get a smile out of anyone who eats it. You feel proud that it's yours and you made it. And you should!

What Should My Signature Dish Be?

Your signature dish should be something you enjoy eating. You may be the only one there to eat it sometimes. If you enjoy eating it, you will enjoy experimenting with the preparation, spices and presentation.

A signature dish needs to be something that starts as raw or fresh ingredients. What you do with those ingredients does not have to be complicated, but it should be tasty when you're done.

What food do you like to eat when you go out to a nice restaurant? What food does your family enjoy? What food do you know you can cook for others that they will enjoy? Maybe it was your mother or grandmother's signature dish before you.

If you cannot come up with a dish, I'll suggest that the grill is man's turf. Steaks, burgers, pork chops or chicken are all easy to prepare.

Men love steaks or burgers. I'll give the directions for a great steak. I never like to cook a steak without a meat thermometer. Steak is expensive and it needs to be cooked at the right temperature (which is 145 degrees in the center, a nice red medium-rare piece of beef).

A good steak starts with a good piece of meat. Your finished product cannot be any better than your raw ingredients. Ribeye, T-bone, tenderloin and New York strip steaks are the most tender steaks. They are also the most expensive.

About 20 minutes before grilling, remove the steaks from the refrigerator and let sit, covered, at room temperature. Heat your grill to high. Brush the steaks on both sides with oil and season liberally with salt and pepper. Place the steaks on the grill and cook until two minutes then turn 45 degrees to get the good grill char marks. After two more minutes, flip the steak. If you have a meat thermometer *(if you don't, get one!),* grill until 140 degrees in center. If not, cook 2 more minutes, and then pull from the grill.

Now, the most important part, and the part most people don't do. Let the meat rest for 5 minutes. Put foil over the steaks and allow the meat juices to re distribute themselves in the steak. This will be the difference between your meat tasting great or being nice and juicy and tasting great!

As you learn to cook a steak, you may choose to add a dollop of butter or a bit of blue cheese on top of the steak. You may add sautéed mushrooms or garlic as a compliment.

Soon you'll be learning how to make baked potatoes or grilled sweet potatoes and brussel sprouts or asparagus to your meal. You'll be on your way to cooking an entire signature meal!

Just like any skill, cooking takes practice.

Bon Appétit! (French – means *Enjoy your meal*)

21

Rub a Dub Dub - How to Wash a Vehicle

(Because the Explorers' main fundraiser each year is a wash-a-thon during which they typically wash 90-110 vehicles, this is an important lesson just prior to the car wash. Whether you have to wash one vehicle or a hundred, though, the technique that follows is still applicable.)

Whether your goal is to keeps your car looking new or just removing road salt, it's a good idea to give your vehicle a bath regularly. It's expensive to use that drive through car wash and it doesn't do near as good of a job as washing by hand. Here's how:

Tools of the Trade

The tools required to wash a vehicle are a water source, hose and spray nozzle, soap and bucket, sponge and brush, and towel or chamois.

You should consider soap products designed specifically for washing cars. They can be found at the local auto parts store or mass merchandiser. Read the directions on the car care products you use. Some might have special tips about how to achieve the best results with that company's products.

Pour an appropriate amount of soap into a bucket and fill with water (warm water is available). If you are using specialty soap, follow instructions. Otherwise regular shampoo is a mild soap that works fine and a cap full in a bucket of water is sufficient. (Don't use your Mom's $300/bottle shampoo. The cheap stuff will work fine!)

Rub a Dub Dub

Before applying any soap to the vehicle, you should rinse the exterior of the car trying to remove all loose dirt and debris. Pay particular attention to any gravel or tiny rocks in mud or dirt that may be on vehicle. If they are not washed off, the pressure of the sponge or brush could cause scratches. Make sure the entire surface of the vehicle is wet before applying a sponge or brush.

Once the vehicle is wet, take soapy brush or sponge and scrub (lightly) the entire surface of the vehicle. This should be done in a systematic way. Wash the car section by section, starting at the top. Let gravity help you. so dirt works its way down the vehicle. Circle around the car several times, washing lower areas with each round.

Scrub your car like you scrub your private parts in the shower. Get it clean, but BE GENTILE!

Scrub the lower body and the wheels last, as these are the dirtiest, grittiest parts and are most likely areas to pick up that small debris that can scratch the paint. It's a good idea to use a separate wash mitt, brush or sponge on the bottom.

Do not let the sponge or brush touch the ground. Be sure to rinse them off regularly. Make certain there is no gravel in the bottom of your soap bucket.

Darker colors are more difficult to get clean and show the dirt more readily. You may have to scrub twice on darker vehicles.

Rinse your entire vehicle thoroughly. Be certain to rinse all soap from body and wheels.

High and Dry

Let your towels do the hard work when you're drying your car. Don't rub your towels so hard on the paint. You'll get streaks. Towels absorb liquid. Just lay a clean, dry towel flat and pat it straight down onto the car, then pull it away. Repeat until the car is dry; you may need several towels to do this properly.

Open the doors, hood, and trunk/hatch when you're drying your car. Wipe all around the edges of these parts. Water gets trapped in these areas, and will run out while you're driving and leave streaks on your paint as it dries. If your grille has slats, wipe each individual slat down as well.

A car is not clean unless it's clean on the inside too. Take the time to detail your interior. Take the floor mats out and vacuum underneath them. Time to toss out those fast food wrappers, vacuum the carpets, use some leather or cloth cleaner on the seats. Hopefully you won't find a half eaten burger or that homework assignment you lost!

Now it's time to go for a ride and show off!

22

Take the Pledge

Leaders are often asked to help with fundraisers. Whether it is a benefit for a new wing on the local hospital or the middle school service club car wash, the success of any fundraiser depends on people's ability to get pledges from others.

Use the right terminology—donations vs pledges

There is a bit of a negative connotation when it comes to the word "donation". Donations are given with nothing or little expected in return.

A pledge is a formal promise on behalf of both the pledgor and the pledgee. The pledgor offers money or other consideration to the pledge who promises to use the money for its intended purpose. It is an informal verbal contract.

Tell your story and be passionate about it!

You need to show passion when you're asking people to pledge. Tell the reason for the project and why you are supporting it. If you're not passionate about the project, you probably should not be taking pledges.

Campaigns with pitch videos are more likely to be successful. You may want to consider a short video explaining the project and connecting with prospective pledgors. Then give people a call to action such as "Find the whole story on my campaign page!" and include the link to your campaign.

Don't let them get you down

Not everyone is going to be on board with your project. That's okay! Focus on the people who are supporting your project and not on those who don't. Spotlight who will benefit from the project in the pitch. Focus on your passion and vision for your project.

If people don't seem to have a sense of urgency and suggest that they'll pledge later, explain the limited time frame in which you will be taking pledges.

Build a community

Supporters want to feel like they're a part of the project so keep them updated with the project and with what you're up to. Let them know how much you appreciate their pledges and maintain an engaged and supportive community even after your campaign.

Thank them

Above all, be sure to show your gratitude for the support others show. A written thank you may be in order. A gracious thanks is important.

The success of any fundraising project usually depends on a few leaders. If you're passionate about the project, get involved and BE A LEADER!

V

Leadership & Stuff

23

With a Goal in Mind

The year I started the Explorers Club, the City of Chamberlain was trying to build a softball/baseball complex and I thought we could help out a bit with that. We talked about it at one of our meetings and the boys liked the idea so I was looking for ways they could raise some money for that project.

One of the Explorers' projects that year was a day trip to Pierre. I knew quite a few public elected officials in our state capital and I knew Governor Bill Janklow. I called and arranged for a visit to his office as part of the itinerary for that day.

Governor Janklow loved kids so when we made the trip to his office on the appointed day, he had all the boys gather around him for a photo. Before the photo, though, he asked the boys about the club.

"What are the Explorers?" asked the governor.

"We help people," came a reply from one of the guys.

"Help them with what?" asked the governor.

"Well we're going to help raise money for baseball and softball fields," one of them erupted.

Janklow nodded and asked, "How much are you going to

raise?".

Now we had not talked about this. I kinda thought we could raise $1,000-1,500. But before I could say anything, one of the kids belted out "FIVE THOUSAND DOLLARS!".

Janklow looked at me and I'm sure I had a surprised look on my face. He got a big smile on his face. He told the guys that if they raised $5,000 by the end of the school year, he would match.

There was an audible "wow" from the group and then spontaneous high fives throughout.

This would certainly test the Explorers and Janklow knew it. I think he also knew that they were capable of it and that they would be successful. He also knew how great they would feel if they could accomplish this working together.

They took the picture with Governor Janklow who had a twinkle in his eye as the shutter captured the moment. The Explorers left his office with the challenge and goal of $5,000 in hand!

The meeting with the governor was in February so we did have three months to work on it. But raising $5,000 would definitely be a challenge.

So what would the Explorers do to raise $5,000. I considered many different ideas but finally presented the idea of a car wash-a-thon to them. They would take pledges for each car they washed.

They agreed that it was a good idea and so we started planning the car wash. About two weeks prior to the car wash, I equipped each Explorer with an envelope with all the information about the car wash on one side and a place to record the pledges on the other side.

For two weeks, the Explorers worked on securing pledges

from friends and family. We publicized the event so that people knew how it worked and what the money was being raised for. The community was very supportive.

The day of the car wash came. It was a nice early May Saturday afternoon. There were cars there when they started the car wash and there were cars still coming six hours later at the end of the cars wash. At the end of the car wash, the boys had washed 69 vehicles.

They raised over $4,000 with tips and pledges. They had raised some money earlier with a middle school dance and autograph and memorabilia auction. So their total surpassed the $5,000 goal.

When we figured out they had raised the money, I called Governor Janklow to tell him. He asked if I could line up a school assembly for the check presentation. He was ready to come down the next day since it was the last day of school for the year.

With the help of Principal Johnson, we arranged for the choir to sing and the band to play at the assembly in front of the entire middle and elementary student body. The mayor and city commissioners were all invited to the assembly.

The governor came to school the next day. When I picked him up at the airport, he had this big check for pictures. But he was careful to ensure I couldn't see it.

So the choir sang and the band played. Then I introduced the Explorers and asked them, to line up in front of the other students. Then Janklow told the story about the Explorers' visit to his office earlier that year. He told everyone that he didn't think they could ever raise $5,000 and that it showed how important a goal was. He talked about how you can do things you don't know you're capable of if you have a goal.

Then he pulled out the check. He told the Explorers that they did such a wonderful job and that he was so proud of their unselfish activities that he was going to give them $10,000 rather than just match their $5,000.

The kids went crazy. The Explorers were high-fiving each other. The governor went down the line of Explorers and gave them each a high five. The students were standing and applauding. The adults present were shocked.The City of Chamberlain had $15,000 for their softball/baseball complex.

They learned the value of setting a goal, worked together as a team and achieved their goal.

Goal Setting

Virtually everyone has goals or things they would like to accomplish or achieve. Formal goal-setting can be an over-whelming task and is the main reason most people do not do it.

There are thousands of books that will tell you how to reach those goals. These few pages are dedicated to breaking goal setting and accomplishment down into a few simple steps to help you start down the path to achieving your goals.

Accomplishing goals may not always be easy, but having goals, whether big or small, is part of what makes life good. It gives us a sense purpose, gives us direction and gets us interested and engaged, all of which are good for our overall happiness.

Decide your goal

Determine what you want to do or work toward. It can be *anything*, as long as it's something you want to do. It should be something that you're interested in and gets you excited or motivated. It can be a big thing or a small thing - sometimes it is easier to get going with something small. It often helps if it's something that challenges you to reach a little bit beyond what you currently can do.

The Explorers didn't need to decide their goal. Governor Janklow did it for them!

Write it down

This may be the most important step in the process. When you write your goals down, you increase you chance of reaching them. Be sure to write down how you will know that you have reached your goal. Write down your deadline. The more specific you are, the better your chance of achieving your goals. Write your goals in terms of what you want, not what you don't want. You want to focus on positive action.

Tell someone

Tell someone you know who will be supportive of your goals. Ask them to encourage you and check on you. Avoid sharing goals with anyone who will not be supportive.

The Explorers didn't need to tell someone because everyone already knew!

Break your goals down

The bigger the goal, the more important it is that you break it down into smaller steps or goals. What are the smaller goals that are steps on the way to achieving your larger objective? Smaller, more specific steps help bring our larger goal into better focus. A goal like "I want to be healthier" will be much easier if we break it down into more specific, smaller goals like "go running three times a week" or "run two miles in fifteen minutes."

It is just as important that you write down your smaller goals and establish deadlines for them. Achieving smaller goals along the way gives you a feeling of success. It also keeps us on track toward our bigger goal.

The Explorers had to break the goals down to how many pledges each would get and how many cars they thought they could wash.

Plan your steps

Have you ever tried to push a car? The hardest part is to get it started. Once rolling, it's easier to keep it rolling. It's the same with goals. Getting started is the hardest part.

You may not know where to start. Your first step might be to do some research. "How to..." is an easy search. Ask someone who has done what you want to do. Perhaps there is a book out there that will help you.

Then think of your next step...and the next...

I helped the Explorers plan their pledging process, their promotion of the car wash and how they would efficiently wash as many cars as possible at the car wash. Each of these needed a precise plan.

Keep going

Sometimes working toward your goals can be difficult or frustrating. If what you are doing isn't working, go back and reconsider your steps. Ask people you know for their ideas on what you could do. They may help you see a different way.

Consider different ways of reaching your goals and you're more likely to be successful. Don't be afraid to take a break and then re-read the goal you wrote down when you started. It's okay to adjust your goal if you need to.

Celebrate

It is so important to celebrate when you reach your goal. Take time to enjoy it and thank those that helped you. Think about what you enjoyed and learned along the way.

The Explorers went to Minneapolis to a pair of Twins games to celebrate their achievements!

Now, what is your next goal or project going to be?

24

Lead, Follow or Get Out of the Way

There are no "born" leaders. Being a leader and developing leadership skills is learned. Some leadership qualities may come easier for some, but all leadership qualities are learned and not innate.

Some people may have a little more confidence in themselves than others. That does not necessarily make them leaders. It has been proven that anyone can learn to be a leader.

Leadership is not telling others what to do. It's more about influencing others by making powerful individual choices. This is one of the most important traits of a leader - the ability to make decisions for yourself, being able to stand up to peer pressure and set a personal standard of behavior.

Leaders and followers step into their roles at a very young age but you can change your path. The question is: "Do I want to be a leader or a follower?"

If you want to be a leader, there are a few simple skills you can work on to develop leadership skills. These skills will empower you with the confidence and tools to make choices for yourself and not have to follow the crowd or cave in to peer pressure.

#1 The Power of a Positive Attitude – A "Leader" says "Yes, I Can!"

There will be many people throughout your life who will tell you why you CAN NOT do or be something. A leader stays focused on maintaining a positive attitude no matter what the people around them say or do. A leader stands up to peer pressure everyday to make choices for themselves.

Tell yourself to say "Yes I can!" even when you are not sure. The first step to being a leader is to always say, "Yes, I Can." Understand how powerful a positive attitude can be!

#2 Overcoming Adversity – A "Leader" says "It's not a problem, it's a Challenge!"

Everyday life is filled with challenges disguised as "problems." Try to recognize these challenges and deal with them as challenges rather than problems.

Try to eliminate the phrase "I Can't" from your vocabulary. Leaders learn very quickly in life that saying "I Can't" is just an excuse not to try. It makes it easy to give up.

There is always another solution. You just need to ask a different or better question to find more solutions. Each challenge in life is an opportunity to learn a new lesson.

Ask better questions and be creative in finding solutions

to life's challenges. Try to find the lesson in each of life's challenges.

#3 Perseverance - A "Leader" says "Never give up, never give up, never give up!"

It is very easy to quit or give up when something gets hard in life. A Leader knows that the easiest path is not always the best path.

When J.K. Rowling's first Harry Potter book was rejected by twelve different publishers, she did not give up. She went to a thirteenth company and got a deal.

Quitting is easy. It's a habit that begins at a young age. It's important to learn at a very young age the power of building positive habits in life.

Understand the power and importance of not quitting and fulfilling their commitments in life. Learn to be persistent and fulfill commitments.

#4 Commitment - A "Leader" says "I may fail or make mistakes BUT I always learn and move ahead!"

Mistakes and failure are an integral part of life. If you've never failed, it's because you've never taken a risk. It is human nature to learn the most in life from our mistakes or failures. Leaders learn to do their best and are not beaten down by their mistakes. Leaders learn to ask themselves a powerful question each time they make a mistake or fail: "What can I learn from this experience?"

It's okay to make mistakes in life as long as you learn and do your best. Strive to find the lesson in each of life's experiences.

#5 Excellence - A "Leader" says "I will always do my best!"

"EXCELLENCE" or doing your very best, is a daily decision. Anyone can be average - the best of the worst or the worst of the best. It takes a focused effort every day to do your best. It really is an attitude. Leaders choose to do their best in everything they do - it becomes their trademark.

I'm sure you know people who always give their best effort when they do something. They may not even like what they are doing but they still do their best.

It's not about being better than other people; it's just about being the best you can be.

Do your own best and do not worry about comparing yourself to other people. It is so important to challenge yourself to do your very best every day.

You can be a great leader. Always lead by example and strive for the best.

A leader does not ask who wants to climb the mountain. If climbing the mountain is the right thing to do, a leader lets others know they are welcome to join him and then climbs, never looking back to see who is following.

There are many great books on leadership. If you want more information on leadership, I recommend:

- Wooden on Leadership by John Wooden & Steve Jamison
- *How to Win Friends & Influence People* by Dale Carnegie
- *Drive: The Surprising Truth About What Motivates Us* by Daniel H. Pink
- *The Seven Habits of Highly Effective People* by Steven R. Covey
- *Developing the Leader Within You* by John C. Maxwell
- *Extreme Ownership: How U.S. Navy SEALs Lead and Win* by Jocko Willink
- *Leaders Eat Last* by Simon Sinek
- *Good To Great* by Jim Collins
- *Principle Centered Leadership* by Stephen Covey
- *The Art of War* by Sun Tzu

25

In Giving We Receive - Servant Leadership

My Dad, Harold W. "Harry" Knust, was civic minded. He started the Chamberlain Chamber of Commerce in 1963. He realized the importance of the community working together. He served on the city commission for nine years. He organized the Chamberlain High School's athletic banquet for many years.

Dad showed me how to serve others long before the Jesuits at Creighton University ever got a hold of me. He taught me about servant leadership.

Servant leadership is a different kind of leadership than traditional leadership. Instead of others working to serve the leaders, the leader exists to serve others.

A servant leader does this by demonstrating:

·Empathy – understanding and sharing the feelings of others

·Listening – not only to the words, but the message as well

·Stewardship - the job of supervising or taking care of something

·Commitment to personal growth of others

The servant leader approaches situations looking to serve

the needs of others, as a servant first! The servant leader seeks to address wants and requirements as their priority, with leadership as a secondary purpose.

In a leader-first perspective, a person aims to gain control quickly often driven by the desire and prospects for material gain or influence.

Where the leader-first dynamic can sometimes tend to appease a personal desire for power, the servant leader looks first to how his service benefits others. Then servant leader's progression to a position of leadership comes after their commitment to service.

True
LEADERS
have a
servant's
heart.
Christine Caine

The servant leader typically encourages their subordinates to look to serve others as their priority over focusing on personal gains. The servant leader looks to share the power that goes along with leadership.

26

Flush the Stinkin' Thinkin'

Growing up is hard. Your peers can be mean and difficult. You have to deal with Instagram likes and Snap scores. You get constant feedback from others which making it difficult to actually listen to yourself. It's easy to embrace negative thoughts.

You know these thoughts:

"I didn't get invited to Julie's party... I'm such a loser."

"I missed the bus... nothing ever goes my way."

"My science teacher wants to see me... I must be in trouble."

"I'm not going to make the basketball team. I'm no good at anything."

You're not alone. Everyone struggles with these thoughts. The question is how do you deal with them. Some of your peers are better at suppressing them than others, but you can be assured that they have to work at portraying that confidence.

Think about what it is that makes you doubt yourself. Some of your friends make you feel good about yourself while other probably make you feel bad. Make an effort to spend more time with them friends that make you feel good about yourself.

Try to be the friend that makes others feel good. Offer a compliment when your friends do something well. Let them know you empathize with them if they have some misfortune. Be the positive force in the relationship and you will soon find that you get that same positivity from your friend.

The best way to be more confident is to focus on the positive aspects of your life. Sometimes you may need help doing that. Be sure to get that help from the people you surround yourself with.

If you find that a friendship sucks the energy from you, perhaps it's time to give that friendship a rest. Avoid those who don't lift you up. After all, are they really a friend if they always bring you down?

Bad things happen to everyone. Don't emphasize or exaggerate these experiences. Don't make them more important than they are. It doesn't always happen to you – even if it feels that way.

If you look around you, you'll find others have unfortunate experiences as well. You're not a victim. Focus on how you can overcome the challenge. Talk to someone who has had the same experience and ask them how they overcame it. Don't get mad at yourself. Handle it – you can!

Don't blame yourself for things you did not do or are not under your control. Sh*t happens! Sometimes we cannot control it. Don't dwell on it. Move forward.

Try to take bad situations and find some positive in them. What can I learn from this? How can I avoid this situation or experience in the future? Help your friends do the same thing.

You are blessed with many talents. You need to focus on them. They may be different talents than your friends possess. That doesn't mean they are lesser skills – just different. Figure out what those talents are and focus on them.

Remember Eeyore in Winnie the Pooh? He is the pessimistic, gloomy, depressed, old grey stuffed-donkey. Eeyore has a negative opinion of the other animals in the forest. He says some of them have no brain at all - only grey fluff. Wow! Let's hang with Eeyore!

Remember Tigger? He's the positive tiger who is full of energy. He is friendly, cheerful, outgoing and has complete confidence in himself. When Tigger introduces himself, he often says the proper way to spell his name and that is "T-I-double-Guh-Er", which spells "Tigger".

Who do you think is more fun to be around? People who are positive are more fun to be around. You'll find people will seek you out to get a positive spin on things. Negativity drains energy from you and those around you. It wears you out.

It's not always easy to be positive. But it is ALWAYS worth it. More realistic and balanced thinking leads to positive action, which, tends to bolster confidence, enhance self-esteem and result in greater happiness.

27

Gratitude is a Great Attitude

Of all the topics I've covered here, perhaps this one is the most important. If you strive for happiness in your life, gratitude is the first step. The happiest and most successful people I know are grateful for their blessings and they live that gratitude every day. Studies tell us that gratitude gives us healthy friendships and family ties. It will cause you to do better academically and experience lower levels of anxiety and depression. Most importantly, grateful people are happy people.

What is gratitude?

True gratitude goes beyond writing thank you notes for gifts you've received (see *Thanks a Million!*). That is a basic social skill that falls under the grateful umbrella. But gratitude is much more than being polite. Gratitude is pausing to notice and appreciate the things that are so easily taken for granted - having a place to live, food, clean water, friends, family, and so many others things. It's pausing a moment to reflect on how fortunate we are. It puts us on a path that leads toward being our best self.

When we make it a habit to feel grateful, it makes us more aware of good things as they happen. Sometimes, feelings of gratitude happen spontaneously. But we also can create feelings of gratitude by deliberately counting our blessings.

The best part is that it is a skill anyone can learn. It's a matter of taking a few minutes each day to look at your situations from a point of appreciation rather than from a deficit. It doesn't take a long time but you can't do it while multi-tasking - you must be focused on this activity alone.

Simply taking two minutes at the end of the day and asking what you are grateful for is great way to get started. This is probably the most difficult part of this entire exercise. It is so easy to get caught up with other things and not find the time for this activity.

Think of relationships (family, friends teachers and others around you), health, experiences, talents, opportunities, and other blessings you have. What are some challenges, failures, conflicts or seemingly bad experiences you had and what positives can you take from them?

Like anything, it may be a struggle at first but you get better at it the more you practice. You may not think you have that many blessings, but when you focus on them, you will realize you are fortunate in so many ways.

After practicing this for a while, you may find yourself recognizing more blessing during the day. You may look out the window and see that the day is ending but there is a beautiful sunset to put an exclamation on that day.

How do I live my gratitude?

Some ways to live your gratitude involve others. You can help someone less fortunate. Don't ask - just do it. This can be a neighbor, grandma, or someone you know who could use a little help. You can volunteer a homeless shelter, soup kitchen or non-profit. Compliment others and let them know what you appreciate about them.

Some ways to live your gratitude involve just you. Look for the positive in every situation - find something positive in frustrating situations. Practice turning complaints in to in to something that you appreciate instead. Look for awe-inspiring moments in your day - sunset, the sound of the baby's laughter, etc. - and share them with others.

These are just a few examples. Once you start, you'll see they are easy to find if you are looking!

Why Gratitude Matters

Gratitude doesn't just feel good, it's good for us! Feeling grateful on a regular basis is a positive emotion that can have a big effect on our lives. Brain research shows that positive emotions are good for our bodies, minds, and brains.

Positive emotions boost our ability to learn and make good

decisions, balance out negative emotions, make us happier, less stressed, and less depressed. When we feel grateful, we might also feel happy, calm, joyful, or loving.

Gratitude leads to positive actions and makes us more likely to do a kindness in return. Your gratitude also can have a positive effect on someone else's actions. Thanking people can make it more likely they'll do a kindness again.

Gratitude helps us create loving bonds, builds trust, and helps us feel closer to others. We build better relationships with gratitude.

Noticing the things you're grateful for is just the first step in building a gratitude habit, but you can try other things too, like taking the time to thank people or pausing to appreciate a star-filled sky. Start now. What's good about this moment?

VI

Digital Stuff

28

Scrubbing the Online You

At some point, you are likely to search for a job. Whether you're striving for summer employment or a career position, there are many things that a prospective employer considers when making a hiring decision.

A resume, interview, and references are all things to stress about when you're trying to find a job. But there are some considerations that are less obvious.

How does your social media history look? Do you know? Have you looked? Make no mistake, employers do look. I know because I have! You would be surprised at what potential employers can find.

119

Social media and your job

Snooping around prospective employee's social media accounts is an easy way for an employer to get some idea about your personal habits - habits that the employer will be taking on if he/she hires you.

Employers look for ways to take you out of the running before investing their time interviewing you, or spending money on background checks. There is a limit to what they can learn from a background check. They don't want to be embarrassed by their employees' behavior whether it is on the job or not.

Rub-a-dub-dub

You can have your social media "cleaned" by a professional, though that can be expensive. It's probably better that you do it yourself.

Facebook is the number one place employers look, followed by Twitter and LinkedIn. Other sites are tougher to connect directly to you, but that doesn't mean that they're "safe." If you put it out there, it can be found. But what exactly is it that employers are looking for?

Red Flags

- Drugs: Bragging about any use of drugs is probably the biggest mistake you can make. Even in places where marijuana is legal, this is a huge red for employers.
- Alcohol: Until you are 21 years, alcohol falls under the category above - it is illegal for you. Once you are of age, you must ask yourself if a stranger were to see this picture or post, what impression would they have of me? Best answer: don't post about your alcohol consumption even when legal.
- Profanity: Whether it's the lyrics from your favorite band or liking a post in which your friend used the f-word as a

noun, verb and adjective in the same sentence, profanity sends a bad message. Get rid of it!

· Friends and Followers: Your friends speak your character. Browse your friends and what do you see? Are they a reflection of the person that you want an employer to consider? Just be honest with yourself. You may want to consider changing your settings to require your permission before you're tagged in something. Check who or what accounts you follow and ask yourself what does that say about you to an employer.

· General Warnings: Consider deleting posts with repeated and severe misspellings or typos. You're thinking you are safe because all of your social media sites are private. What do you think an employer thinks about someone whose social media is all private? Perhaps this person does and says things that they do not want the public to know about. I can tell you that is a red flag.

Employers aren't looking for angels. Social media profiles reveal a "different side" of you than the professional image.

But you don't want to eliminate yourself from contention before you ever get the opportunity to compete. Don't take a chance on your social media image undermining your efforts. Take an honest look at your entire online image and clean it up.

29

The Great Social Media Lie

The dictionary tells us that delete means to "remove or destroy". That would suggest that when you "delete" a post on Facebook, Twitter or Instagram, that the post is gone, removed or obliterated. Snapchat has convinced its users that a snap "disappears like a ghost".

None of this is true!

The posts or "snaps" are not gone. When you send a Snapchat, a direct message, a text message, or any other such communication to a friend, it doesn't go from your device to theirs. It goes from your device to a server, where a copy is made, and a copy is sent to their device. So even if you both delete the message, there's still a copy on a server that neither one of you has access to.

If necessary, people with the proper equipment (law enforcement officials) could take your device, computer, phone or tablet, hook it up to their computer, and likely within five minutes, can have almost every "Snap" or text or message you have ever sent or received, including the deleted ones.

The "deleted" messages are still on your device. You just

can't see them. Once they are out there, you can't get them back. They are out there forever.

It's not just law enforcement who can recapture these messages. Once something is posted on Facebook, Twitter, or Instagram, anyone who can see the item can copy it and share it with other social media users. They can copy the photo or a screen shot and save it forever.

Copied photos, videos, and information can easily be shared in other places. It can be easily be emailed to a third party, uploaded to a different social media website or even printed and shown to others in person.

There really is no guarantee that something that's posted on social media won't remain on the Internet forever, regardless of how long it's allowed to remain on the original poster's account.

Facebook's servers keep backup copies of deleted information for some time after its deletion. Once you upload something to the Internet (including Facebook), you no longer have complete control over what happens to it.

This issue is not limited to Facebook, Instagram, and Twitter. These are just the most popular. The same issue exists for users of LinkedIn, Pinterest and other popular social media sites.

Be careful what you post. Before posting, ask yourself if you want this post "out there" forever. Could it someday be used against you? Could a prospective college or employer view it negatively? What's the worst that could happen if you did post it? What's the worst that could happen if you didn't post it?

30

ICYMI: You Should F2F That "Important" Text

No one seems to use the telephone anymore. Many people no longer even have a landline phone in their home. Mobile only. Face to face conversation? Forget it! Not happening.

Texting has replaced many traditional forms of communication. Texting is very convenient and is used by all ages.

Texting does present some unique challenges though. Misinterpretation of words, incomplete messages and etiquette issues can cause texting problems.

Here are some things to think about before sending your thumbs into a blur...and hitting "SEND".

Who?

Who is the text message going to? You need to consider that as you compose the message. The style and language you use with your friends may be inappropriate for your parents, co-workers or employer. Be sure your text message is appropriate for your audience.

Don't use LOL and other text slang when it doesn't make sense. Consider who you're texting because many people don't have a clue what ROTFL or SMH mean.

Clear as mud

When you text, the receiver cannot see facial expressions or body language. These non-verbal cues are a key aspect of how your message is received. Because of this, you must exhibit special care in crafting your message so that the receiver understands it as you intended.

You do not want the receiver to be confused as to what you are trying to say. If the message is misinterpreted, you could be on you way to a communication problem – which can lead to bigger problems! Read your message to make sure it is clear before hitting the "send" button.

Let me get back to you on that – promptly

When someone texts you, they assume you will receive the message and immediately respond. Unless you are unavailable, respond quickly. A lack of response can be taken as a lack of caring. If you can't attend to the text message quickly, apologize for your tardiness as soon as you can.

When in doubt, leave them out

Save the smiley faces for your friends. On occasion emojis have their place when sending a text. As a rule though, leave them out. They do not replace the non-verbal communication mentioned above. Generally, it's inappropriate to litter your message with smiley faces.

Don't use text slang unless you know what it means, either. I knew someone who thought LOL stood for "lots of love" rather than "laugh out loud," so when he repeatedly texted LOL to his friend whose father had died, you can imagine the friend's dismay.

Get to the point

Don't be long winded. Don't reply to a two-word text with paragraphs upon paragraphs in your response. If you receive a two-word text from someone, assume that the sender is in a hurry, does not have much time available, or needs a quick response. If you need to go into detail, pick up the phone instead or meet in person.

It's over already

Be aware when the other person is ready to stop texting, and do not try to continue with texts like "Are you still there?" or "Why aren't you responding?" The other person may have been interrupted. End it and move on.

Don't hit send

If you're going back and forth with your friend trying to make plans and you're both being indecisive, save yourself the time and trouble and call them.

Texting a "thank you" note is not OK. You should always call, send a physical card via snail mail or send an e-card.

If it's a work related issue, definitely get in the habit of formulating a concise, grammatically-correct email.

Don't ever text about death or serious illness. Conversations like these require emotion, nuance, and support. They are too fragile to risk being misunderstood or accidentally skipped over.

Don't confuse someone who you've been on only a few casual

dates with by including them in mass texts. It can get awkward, fast.

If you're on the verge of having a serious conversation (like a break up) with a girlfriend, pick up the phone and call first – and if you really want to show some fortitude, tell her in person.

Safety first

Don't text while eating or drinking with others unless you can talk about what you're texting, or it's an emergency. If it's the latter, excuse yourself and handle the situation.

Never text while another person is speaking, unless it is extremely important. If you do have to text, offer a brief explanation immediately so you don't hurt their feelings. Consider excusing yourself if you don't want to share your private details.

If you are tempted to text while walking, don't do it. Step to the side and text out of harms (and other people's) way.

Don't text someone who you know is driving. You do not want to be responsible for them getting in an accident. And, for that matter, don't text while you are driving!

If you're not careful, texting gaffes can be embarrassing and can cause confusion and frustration with friends and clients alike.

VII

Clothing & Stuff

31

Common Scents

Men wear cologne for a variety of reasons – personal branding, favorable first impressions, social benefits in interactions with others, or just to smell good. There are, however, some guidelines for wearing cologne.

When to wear cologne?

If you need to take a shower, cologne won't help you. Besides, water is cheaper than cologne so take a shower and save your money. After you shower, you can wear some cologne.

Quality fragrances are expensive so you may want to be a bit selective about when you wear them. When you are going to be around the ladies, you may want to wear a fragrance. Guys don't appreciate them, you can save your money when you're just hanging with the guys.

What cologne to wear

Good fragrances are complex and change in smell. What you smell when you apply will be different from what the fragrance is later. That is because of the manner in which cologne is made and because of your body chemistry.

While it is nice to get a quality bottle of cologne as a gift, the best person to choose your fragrance is you. Others may reinforce the decision you make but studies show that you are the best one to make the choice. You can do your homework and make a suggestion before Christmas or your birthday. Parents and grandparents are always looking for gift ideas. Let them know what fragrance you like!

You can go to a department store and test a fragrance. Apply some cologne (as suggested below). Then wait! The fragrance will change over then next couple hours. You won't really know unless you wait that long. That means it will be hard to test more than one fragrance per trip to the mall!

How to buy cologne

Colognes come in many different sizes. Smaller bottles usually match the budget better and also come with less risk. If you decide you don't like the fragrance or would like to wear something different, you don't have as much invested in a smaller bottle.

You don't know how often you will be wearing it, and your tastes will probably change once you get the chance to smell different scents. Fragrances do not have an unlimited life span. Changes in temperature and light kill them so it's best to store them in cool, dark places. A bedroom closet or bathroom cupboard is much better than a window sill.

How to wear cologne?

We've all been around someone who wears too much cologne. The scent can be overwhelming and hard to take. It's better to wear no fragrance than too much. You'll always be remembered as the person who doesn't know how to wear cologne.

You should spray cologne on dry skin, preferably after a shower. It should be sprayed 3-6 inches from the skin. Start with a single spray on your chest. Later, you can try other areas.

It is best to apply fragrance to heat areas like your chest, neck, lower jaw, wrist, forearm, inner elbow, shoulder. Your body heat will push the scent throughout the day. Do not spray on all these points at the same time; start with one and then as you learn the scent, spray 2-3 other spots.

Don't rub the cologne into the skin. Don't spray it on your clothes. If you are applying cologne from a regular bottle, take one finger and press it against the opening of your bottle and then tip it over gently. Dab onto the parts of the body described above.

Less is more. Fragrance should be discovered, not announced. People who are close by should be able to smell your cologne, but not be overpowered by it.

32

Tying the Knot

Every man needs to know how to tie a tie. Clip on ties are just not acceptable. Period. Tying a tie once then leaving it tied so you can slip it over your head is a great way to ruin a tie (and just not very manlike!).

Neckties are designed to be tied each time they are worn. There is a certain satisfaction that goes with tying your tie in a nice knot as well.

Despite the fact that there are more than twenty different knots that can be used on a tie, either one of the two knots here will work very well. You only need to know one of them.

Four in Hand Knot

This is first knot many men learn so it is sometimes called the "schoolboy knot". It's the most popular tie knot because it is so simple to tie and is appropriate for most occasions.

- Hang the tie around your collar with the seam facing in and the thick end on your left, 2-3 inches lower than your desired finishing position. You will learn how long to start each end as you become more proficient at tying your tie.

- Bring the thick end horizontally (longer end) across the front of the narrow end, and then pass it back horizontally behind the narrow end. Pass the thick end again across the front of the knot from left to right.
- Now pass the thick end again behind the knot horizontally from right to left. Slip a finger under this second horizontal loop.
- Bring the tip of the thick end up underneath the loop around your collar and feed it up behind the knot, down over the front of the knot and through that third horizontal loop. Pull the thick end through the horizontal loop and snug it down.
- Adjust the tie by holding the knot in one hand and pulling gently on the narrow end with the other.

Windsor Knot

Sometimes known as the Full Windsor knot or Double Windsor knot, the Windsor knot is a larger knot with a symmetrical triangular shape. It is often mistaken as being difficult to tie. The loops which form the back of the knot allow a bit of space between the collar and the necktie making the Windsor comfortable to wear.

- Hang the tie around your collar with the seam facing inward and the thick end on your left, 3-6 inches lower than your desired finishing position. You will learn how long to start each end as you become more proficient at tying your tie.
- Cross the wide end horizontally in front of the slim end.
- Tuck the wide end up and beneath the loop around your

neck, coming out point-upward behind the knot. Use one finger to hold the knot in place.

· Pull the wide end all the way down.
· Bring the wide end around behind the knot and pass it horizontally from right to left.

· Flip the wide end tip up and tug it diagonally across the front of the knot.
· Loop the wide end over the top of the loop around your collar and bring it back down. It should emerge on the left of the thin end.
· Bring the wide end horizontally across the front of the knot,

from left to right. This forms a horizontal band. Tuck a finger through it and hold it in place.

- Bring the wide end underneath the loop one more time, around the collar with the tip aiming up.
- Turn the wide end down and slide the tip through the horizontal loop you saved with your finger in step 8.
- Pull the wide end all the way down and smooth out any creases or slack in the knot.

The length of a tie when tied is an important part of the style of a tie. The front of the tie should come just past the top of the waist of your pants. The back length of the tie should be tucked into the flap on the back side of the front length and should not show. So it should be just a little shorter than the front length.

This is important. Nothing says I don't know how to wear a tie like the wrong length even if you can tie a great knot. As mentioned above, it may take a little practice to get your length right.

Ladies love dimples!

Another important detail in tying a tie is the dimple which creates a look of sophistication that finishes the overall portrait of your neck-wear. A tie dimple is a slight indentation in the fabric of your tie just below the knot.

You can create a dimple under the knot in your necktie by gently pressing in with your index finger. Pinch the sides of the knot with your thumb and middle finger and squeeze them together as you pull the knot tight.

Try both knots. See which you like better. Always remember that with any knot, a little practice is all it takes to become a real expert at tying your tie in no time.

A tie alone does not make a well-dressed man. What you wear with that tie is important as well and is covered in the next chapter.

33

More Than a Tie

Now that you know how to tie your tie, you need to consider what to wear with it. A tie alone does not make you a well-dressed man. In fact, if you wear the wrong clothing with your tie, you'd be better off not wearing the tie at all.

In high school, you may be asked to wear a tie for a variety of events. Fine arts, sports, and other extra-curricular activities are common occasions to be asked to wear a tie. You may not be asked to wear a sport coat or blazer but don't be afraid to do so. A jacket really gives a finished look.

If the shirt fits...

The most important thing to consider when wearing a tie is your dress shirt. It must fit you well. A tie is not uncomfortable but a tie worn with a shirt with a neck that is too small is uncomfortable. Make sure your shirt fits!

Get a button-down long sleeve oxford shirt. You should comfortably be able to put two fingers inside the collar when it is buttoned. The sleeve should come down to the small knobby bone on the outside of the wrist. Long sleeve shirts are not any warmer than short sleeve and look a hundred times better!

Here is a simple rule for your shirt: wear white or light blue. Yes other colors work, but you aren't going to have a closet full of dress shirts. Start with white and you can add light blue later.

You should have a plain white t-shirt to wear under your dress shirt. Not only does it protect your dress shirt and make it last longer, it makes a white dress shirt look whiter. It provides a finished look.

You can wear any color tie with either of these (no white tie with white shirt; no light blue tie with light blue shirt). These are the most versatile shirt colors. Choose a tie that contrasts well with your shirt.

Slacks no jeans

Jeans and cargo pants don't work with a tie. Period. Your best bet is a pair of tan, dark blue or black khakis. These colors offer the most flexibility. Your pants or slacks should not be baggy and should be worn just below the navel. You should wear a belt with your slacks or pants.

Hard soled leather shoes with black or navy socks are the appropriate footwear to compliment a tie. No sneakers! A nice pair of black or brown loafers will serve you well. Your shoes and belt should be the same color. Think of that when you are shopping.

A tie bar, clasp, tack or chain may be worn to help keep tie in place. Place it between your third and fourth shirt buttons and be sure the bar or pin is fastened to both the tie and the placket of your shirt.

Follow these simple rules the next time you wear a tie and you'll look great.

List of Explorers 2001-2024

MAN STUFF - THINGS A YOUNG MAN NEEDS TO KNOW

Anthony Allgood	Jacob Byre	Jazz Dominguez	Tyler Frederick
Dalton Andera	Sam Byers	Dylan Dominiack	Davey Freidel
Levi Andera	Josh Cadwell	Eli Donovan	David Frewaldt
Colton Anderson	Cameron Caldwell	Maximillian Donovan	Ethan Friesz
Devyn Anderson	Phil Carlson	Sawyer Donovan	Seth Friesz
Dilen Anderson	Ami Carpenter	Xavier Donovan	Alex Garcia
Ian Anderson	Cameron Carpenter	Derrick Dorman	James Geppert
Chris Arbach	Davis Carson	Brant Douville	Maddex Gilman
Justin Arcoren	Donovan Carson	Estan Douville	Conner Graves
Luke Baker	Brad Champagne	John Dunn	Gavin Graves
Michael Baldwin	Delante Charger	Hunter Eimers	Brant Gullickson
Caleb Barnett	Austin Cheney	Nick Endres	Dawson Gullickson
Casey Barnett	Adam Chernotik	Carl Estes	Rayden Haak
Gage Basting	Chuck Chernotik	Desme Estes	Kyle Haiar
Jade Basting	Dustin Chernotik	Jacey Estes	Landon Hall
Michael Baukus	Gavin Chipps	Hayden Evans	Tanner Hall
Skyler Bertram	Jarrid Claussen	Jett Evans	Hayden Handel
Gabe Big Eagle	Nick Claussen	Parker Evans	Trevor Hanig
Jerome Big Eagle	Alex Crawford	Taivin Fallis	Jack Hanzlik
Justice Big Eagle	Chance Crazy Bull	Adrian Farmer	William Hanzlik
Cole Black Crow	Andrew Cruz	William Fast Dog	Breckyn Harmon
Chance Blum	Jackson Cutt	Morgan Fast Wolf	Garrett Harmon
Chisum Blum	Lucas Daly	Brock Feltman	Kolton Harris
Jeff Bode	Mason Daly	Evan Fleury	Thomas Hawk
Josh Bordeaux	Paul Day	Tyson Fleury	Jacob Heron
Brady Bunker	Ben Defender	Torell Flute	Cole Hickey
Ashton Burke	Peter Delgado	Hunter Foltz	Connor Hickey
Noah Bury	Matt Denke	Kyle Forester	Gunner Hickey

Ian Hickey	Matt Johnson	Brian Madison	Dakota Munger
Lane Hickey	Mike Johnson	Mason Mahnke	Jake Mutziger
Ryker Hickey	Tate Johnson	William Mahnke	Brody Neilen
Tayn Hickey	Kannon Jones	Braiden Mahrt	Trey Neilan
Wade Hickey	Rain Jones	Rich Marone	Zack Nelson
Wyatt Hickey	Maxwell Kelsey	Joden Matthews	Jozie Nesladek
Joe Hieb	Garrett Kirkpatrick	Colin Mayer	Jozy Nesladek
Christian Hoffer	Spencer Kirkpatrick	Sheldon Mayer	David Newton
Brett Holm	Isaiah Knife	Kenyon McClosky	Mitchell Old Lodge
Shane Holmquist	Dodge Knippling	Connor McKee	Grady Olson
Chase Hopkins	Hunter Knippling	Sean McManus	Jordan Pasion
Aadyn Hosek	Alex Knust	Sellyck McManus	Jacob Peterson
Zach Hough	Blaine Krenke	Andy McQuistion	Memphis Peterson
Matthew Houke	Michael Krogstad	Clinton McQuistion	Zach Peterson
Morgan Houke	Derek Kutil	Demarius Medicine Crow	Carson Powell
London Houska	Tyson Langdeau	Wakinyan Mesteth	Collin Powell
Adam Hutmacher	Jarred Larson	Dennis Metcalf	Connor Powell
Austin Hutmacher	Ben LeBrun	Antonio Middletent	Nathan Powell
Caden Hutmacher	Skyler Leiferman	Mike Mildt	Thomas Powell
Nash Hutmacher	Ethan Lein	Charlie Miller	Carson Powers
Noah Hutmacher	Andrew Lepkowski	Hayes Miller	Sutton Powers
Karter Hyland	James Lien	Levi Miller	Wyatt Powers
Kolby Hyland	Jacob Lopez	Josh Miranda	Brandon Priebe
Casey Iversen	Jake Lopez	Oyate Monje	Drayton Priebe
Nathan Iverson	Lucas Lopez	Joe Mousseau	Hudson Priebe
Brandon Jensen	Tino Lopez	Cooper Mueller	Michael Priebe
Damon Johnson	Troy Lopez	Eric Mueller	Riggs Priebe

145

Tiegen Priebe	Marc Schwenk	Cody Stein	Ronin Urban
Traxton Priebe	Matthew Schwenk	Luke Stewart	Josh Valandra
Alan Provost	Tayeden Seeking Land	Jason Stone	Chris Viereck
Nathan Rademacher	Daniel Selland	Deion Stork	Neil Viereck
Mason Red Wing	Ian Sharpe	Bryken Storms	Nick Wall
Tommy Redig	Caden Sharping	Eric Strande	Thaddeus Weisenbaugh
Caleb Reimer	Jeff Shaw	Brennan Swanson	Mato Wells
David Renbarger	Isaac Shepherd	Brooks Swanson	Mikyle Weston
Eric Reuer	Jason Shields	Jack Swanson	Elye White Mouse
Garrett Ristau	Joseph Sims	Thomas Swanson	Sandler Wiekamp
Gunner Ristau	Michael Sinkie	Keith Sweet	Chris Willrodt
Zach Ristau	Tayvin Sitting Bear	Michael Sweet	David Willrodt
Race Roberts	Everardo Skunk	Andy Taecker	River Willrodt
Remington Rossow	Cody Smith	Devin Taylor	Lance Wind
Anthony Salinas	Ryan Smith	John Thelen	Kevin Wingert
Devin Santana	William Smith	Eden Thigh	Tim Yeaton
Carter Santiago	Tyler Sorensen	Keshaume Thigh	C.J. Yost
Dominic Santiago	Cruz Soulek	Cannon Thomas	Ethan Zephier-Rich
Loren Sazue	Jackson Soulek	Isaac Thomas	
Lucas Saxton	Cannon Speer	Stevie Thomas	
Michael Schoenfelder	Marques Standing Cloud	Brendan Thompson	
Ryan Schoenhard	Ethan Steckelberg	Colin Thompson	
Cody Schreiber	Jacob Steckelberg	Zack Toering	
Cody Schumacher	Matt Steckelberg	Taran Toupal	
Wyatt Schumacher	Cody Steen	Joe Tyrell	
Chris Schwartz	Kelby Steen	Max Tyrell	
Mike Schwartz	Kooper Steilen	Sam Tyrell	

About the Author

In addition to 20 years with the Explorers Club, Doug Knust drew on 30+ years of fatherhood, 30+ years of teaching religious education (25+ of which was teaching junior high boys) and 25+ years of coaching young men in writing this book.

Knust is a franchised automobile dealer and small business-man and graduated from Creighton University with a finance degree in 1982.

Knust loves to hunt, golf, sail and bicycle. He's a political junkie and is interested in all things finance. He has a bourbon collection. He a life long college basketball fan.

He and his wife, Judy, have three grown children and one granddaughter.

You can connect with me on:

- http://manstuffbook.com
- https://twitter.com/ManStuffBook
- https://www.facebook.com/ReadManStuff
- https://www.instagram.com/TheManStuffBook
- http://dougknust.com

Made in the USA
Coppell, TX
29 November 2024

41288672R00089

Resources

Phillips, David A, PHD. (1992). The Complete Book of Numerology Discovering the Inner Self. Hay House, Inc.

Russ. (2019). It's All In Your Head. HarperCollins.

Russ ON: Delusional Self-Confidence & How To Start Manifesting Your Dream Life, Jay Shetty Podcast, 3 May, 2021, https://youtu.be/-4c61A2VD8k

Victor, Ata Owaji. (21 December, 2020). Oprah Opens Up About The One Role She 'Wanted More Than Anything', Elle. https://www.elle.com/uk/life-and-culture/a35029381/oprah-the-color-purple-role/

Watts, Wallace C. (2015). The Science of Getting Rich. John Rose Publishing.

Winfrey, Oprah. What Oprah Learned From Jim Carrey. Oprah's Life Class, Oprah Winfrey Network, 12 October 2011, https://www.oprah.com/oprahs-lifeclass/what-oprah-learned-from-jim-carrey-video

Made in United States
Orlando, FL
25 September 2024

51969949R00163